Creative CRAZY PATCHWORK

by Helen Moore & Theresia Stockton

A J.B. Fairfax Press Publication

CONTENTS

CONTENTS

EDITORIAL
Managing Editor: Judy Poulos
Editorial Assistant: Ella Martin
Editorial Coordinator: Margaret Kelly
Photography: Andrew Payne
Styling: Kathy Tripp
Illustrations: Lesley Griffith

DESIGN AND PRODUCTION
Production Manager: Anna Maguire
Design: Jenny Nossal
Cover Design: Jenny Pace
Production Artist: Lulu Dougherty
Design Manager: Drew Buckmaster

Published by J.B. Fairfax Press Pty Limited
80-82 McLachlan Ave
Rushcutters Bay NSW, 2011 Australia
A.C.N. 003 738 430
Web: http://www.jbfp.com.au
Email: info@jbfp.com.au

Formatted by J.B. Fairfax Press Pty Limited

Printed by Toppan Printing Company,
Singapore
© J.B. Fairfax Press Pty Limited 1998
This book is copyright. No part may be
reproduced by any process without the
written permission of the publisher. Enquiries
should be made in writing to the publisher.

JBFP 471

CREATIVE CRAZY PATCHWORK
ISBN 1 86343 298 1

DISTRIBUTION AND SALES
Australia: J.B. Fairfax Press Pty Limited
Ph: (02) 9361 6366; Fax: (02) 9360 6262
USA: Quilters' Resource Inc.
2211 North Elston Ave
Chicago 60614
Ph: (773) 278 5695; Fax: (773) 278 1348

ABOUT THE AUTHORS

HELEN MOORE

The eldest of five children, I was taught to sew by my mother when I was a child. Learning to drive her old Elna at about age eight or nine, I was making most of my own clothes by high school. An argument with a needlework teacher over the relevance of cross-stitched gingham tablemats was a minor disruption. Asked to choose a sewing machine for my twenty-first birthday present, I selected one with very few fancy stitches: embroidering clothes wasn't a factor in those days. I completed a teaching degree at Macquarie University and kept sewing for myself. When the time came, I made my wedding dress, bridesmaid's dress, my two sisters' outfits and the boys' bow ties.

The birth of my first daughter (and the drop from two incomes to one) led me to embroidery. I wanted to dress my daughter in pretty smocked and embroidered dresses – but at a reasonable cost. Starting with little bits on dresses and romper suits, I was soon hooked, so I borrowed books from the library and taught myself. Being left-handed, I had to do quite a bit of fiddling until I could figure out how to interpret instructions that were written for right-handers. A second daughter gave me twice the reasons to embroider.

Meeting Theresia through a mutual friend, I was introduced to an expanded world of embroidery (later, I was to find a kindred crazy spirit – or should that be a crazy kindred spirit?). One day I saw a quilt in a sewing shop. It was a Grandmother's Fan with a difference. Made of old ties and heavily embroidered, it was the most wonderful thing I had ever seen. I could drive a sewing machine and I had mastered the basic embroidery stitches – I just had to have a go.

The evening jacket was my first crazy patchwork project – I've never been one to start small! I showed it to Theresia and . . . well the rest is history.

THERESIA STOCKTON

Sewing seems to have been part of me for as long as I can remember. I used to sit under my mother's treadle sewing machine and play with the discarded materials that fell to the floor. I made myself little dollies and clothes for them. I suppose they must have been very primitive creations, but with the praise and encouragement of my mother, I felt that I had created masterpieces.

My family moved from Croatia to Austria, where I received my education. Even though it was wartime, my life and that of my five brothers seemed peaceful and untroubled. I don't recall any sewing activities at that time; I suppose just surviving would have kept my mother busy. In 1949, when I was seventeen, our whole family came to Australia.

At nineteen I married a teacher and, between transfers to the Blue Mountains, Narrandera, Port Macquarie and Cowra, raised four children. At that time, I sewed clothes mainly for the children. Gradually, as the family grew, sewing pursuits became less utilitarian and I began to have time to experiment with fabric, texture and design. Most things I have learnt through trial and error, and have improved my techniques through persistence, research, observation and the advice of like-minded friends.

A satisfying and very positive aspect of my sewing is the way in which I have been able to share my hobby with others. I love to teach sewing, and also enjoy learning new techniques. As a member of both the Quilters' and Embroiderers' Guilds, I am continually supported and stimulated by being surrounded by very creative and generous craftswomen. Sewers are like gardeners – they love to share.

The urge to tackle a new project has been there for a while. Helen and I toyed with the idea of writing a book for some time, but neither of us realised just what we were letting ourselves in for. Now that it's done, we're delighted with the results and hope it will encourage others to try and enjoy crazy patchwork.

INTRODUCTION

It is generally accepted that crazy patchwork has its origins in Victorian times, when extravagance in decoration was at its height. In the years since, its popularity has waned, and those who appreciated crazy patchwork certainly did not make their feelings public. The mid- to late 1980s saw a resurgence in handcrafts of all kinds, possibly hand in hand with Australia's interest in things historical, or maybe it came as some sort of backlash against the plastic mass-production madness of the 70s and early 80s.

Whatever the reason, handcrafts are now not only fashionable again, but those who enjoy them no longer fear being considered second-rate because they made things rather than bought them. All forms of needlecrafts are now undergoing a rebirth. Young women are asking Granny for stitching lessons, and those who no longer have a grandmother are taking classes, joining groups and borrowing or buying books.

Crazy patchwork gives those interested in the fabric arts the very best of all worlds. The strictness of the traditional patchwork where points were required to meet precisely is gone. The urge to embroider on things not generally embroidered can be fulfilled, and the desire to have fun with colour is really satisfied.

We have not tried to set out here the history of crazy patchwork. What we have done is try to give those interested some starting points. For the beginner we set out the basics: how to play with colours and find combinations you like, how to patch the fabric, the stitches to embroider over the seams, the stitch combinations we like to use and some further decoration ideas. We have collected a range of projects that we hope will provide beginners with a starting point, and experienced crazy patchworkers with some fresh ideas.

Because Helen is left-handed and encountered the usual left-handed problems when stitching, we have included instructions for left-handers. Nothing so glib as 'hold your diagrams up to the mirror', but illustrated step-by-step instructions on how to complete the basic stitches used in this book. We hope these will be useful for the 'lefties' among you.

Crazy patchwork is fun. It allows complete freedom of expression, using fabric and thread instead of paints. We hope you will enjoy this book.

Best wishes and crazy good times
Helen and Theresia

MATERIALS

FABRIC

The wonderful thing about crazy patchwork is that you are never confined to a particular kind of fabric. Gone is the 'all pure cotton' rule of the traditional patchworker and quilter. You choose the fabrics depending on the project and the look you're after – shiny silks and satins for evening jackets, velvets for hats, cottons for toys or a mix of them all. It's your choice – be adventurous. Here are a few things to keep in mind when you are selecting your fabrics:

• Think about the ultimate use of the project. Will it ever be washed? A photo album cover won't.

• If it's an article of clothing, consider where it will be worn – the office or a cocktail party.

• If it's a toy that will be played with (very carefully and gently we hope), is it likely to need the occasional sponge wipe to keep it fresh?

• Are you after a comfy-cottage look for your cushions or something more glamorous and sophisticated?

FABRIC TYPES

Pure cotton patchwork fabric is available in the most wonderful range of colours – plain and patterned. It's easy to find, easy to work with, shopkeepers will sell small amounts, it washes and irons well, coordinating colours and patterns are easy to acquire, many designs are available with either gold or silver overstamping, and seasonal designs are available. You could work only with pure cottons and never exhaust the available selection.

Polycotton is a lightweight material, easy to work with and available in a wide range of colours and patterns. Scraps left over from other sewing projects are very useful.

Silk looks fabulous in evening wear and special-occasion pieces. It is available in a variety of weights and textures (slub, raw, dupion etc). Silk frays easily and quickly, so any exposed seams or edges need to be secured with an additional row of machine-stitching or a fray-stopping product.

Satin is delightfully shiny yet still smooth and is fun to include in evening pieces. It also frays easily and should be treated as for silk in this regard. Satin comes in a variety of weights (the cost is indicative here) and a good colour range.

Crepe tends to 'move about', so stitching it to other fabrics, or other fabrics to crepe, should be done with care. A very light iron-on interfacing, attached carefully, often helps to correct this problem. Plain and patterned crepes are available.

Velvet, or the less costly velveteen, is lovely to work with. It is available in strong jewel colours, sometimes with a metallic pattern stamped onto the surface. It can cause the seams to be heavy, so be sure to clip out under the seams to avoid extra bulk.

Lamé and lurex fray, so treat them like silk or satin. The fabrics are fairly fine and fragile and need to be handled with care. Lamé and lurex help to give a sparkle to crazy patchwork pieces.

Lace gives a very soft, feminine look to a piece. It needs to have a lining fabric sewn in with it or the base cloth shows through. Choose a matching or contrasting colour for the lining fabric.

Furnishing fabric can provide a subtle texture, shine or colour pattern that is not available in dress fabrics. Lots of great colours and patterns are available. Look for remnants or superseded sample books.

BASE CLOTH FABRIC

Base cloth fabrics need to be stable but lightweight. Remember, when you are adding the embroidery you will have to sew through the base cloth as well as the fancy fabrics. Lightweight polycottons, calico or sheeting are all suitable. Some crazy patchworkers use their 'uglies' (fabric you thought you liked when you bought it or were given when Aunt Maude cleaned out her sewing cupboard). As long as the fancy fabric you are using is not see-through, you can get away with all sorts of things underneath. Make sure you select a light-coloured base cloth fabric when you work with light-coloured fancy fabrics.

In order that you get maximum impact from your crazy patchwork, try to consider placement when you are piecing your base cloth. Separate patterns and textures from plains. The visual impact of each fabric will be greater if it is not competing with its neighbour. There will be times when placing pattern next to pattern may be unavoidable. If this happens, use a plain braid or lace on the seam to act as a divider and so allow each fabric to look its best.

The following three terms will appear regularly throughout the instructions for the projects in this book:

'Plain fabric' is just that: one colour, no design, no texture.

'Patterned fabric' has a design on the surface or woven into the fabric. The pattern can be floral, checks (plaids) or abstract. The pattern can be printed in different colours on the surface of the fabric, or it can be woven into the fabric.

'Textured fabric' has a 'feelable' surface. This tactile effect can be as a result of the type of threads used in weaving the fabric (such as in slub fabrics) or the weaving technique itself (such as in velvet).

LACES AND BRAIDS

The use of braid and/or lace is a personal choice. Some people just don't like lace and won't use it, others love it and use lots – it's your choice.

Rather than go into details of the kinds of lace that are available, we suggest you consider the following:

• The 'weight' of the lace should complement the project.

• The colour of the lace should tie in with the overall colour scheme. Sometimes cream lace looks less stark than white and this change can be achieved by dipping lace in black tea till it reaches the desired colour.

• Stay away from cheap nylon lace; cotton lace looks much nicer and is available in a selection of widths, weights and patterns.

• A dab of clear nail polish will stop the ends of the lace fraying while you sew it to your project. Remember to tuck the ends into the seams.

• Lace motifs are readily available and look lovely sewn over a plain piece of fabric.

• All of the above considerations apply equally to the various kinds of braid that are available.

BUTTONS, BAUBLES AND BEADS

BUTTONS

Plastic buttons come in a wide range of colours, sizes and shapes. Look for very small plain white, cream or clear buttons to form flowers or flower centres. Try small flower-shaped ones and, for children's projects, look for fancy buttons depicting children and their interests.

Metal buttons do not come in as big a range as plastic ones. Basically they only come in gold, silver and brass. Some can be used for flowers, and an increasing range of fancy buttons that can be used in place of charms.

Mother-of-Pearl buttons are magnetic to crazy patchworkers. We are drawn to them. Use old buttons in projects where an aged look is desired, or try some of the lovely, shaped ones (hearts etc) that are now available.

Wood and bone buttons are often too big for small crazy patchwork projects, but they look wonderful on country-style pieces.

BEADS

Glass or crystal beads give a lovely sparkle to crazy patchwork projects. Glass beads also come in a huge range. They are usually quite expensive, but for special pieces or where an exact colour is required, they may be the better choice.

Plastic beads come in a huge variety of sizes, shapes and colours. They add sparkle and glamour.

Wooden beads, like wooden buttons, look particularly good on country-style pieces.

Metal beads (or metallised plastic) come in a large size and shape range.

Look out for some of the many other types of beads available.

BAUBLES

Into this category fall things like charms, tassels, iron-on or stitch-on motifs and fringing. The best thing about crazy patchwork is that you are not restrained by rules of what to add by way of decoration. Our rule has become: 'if it takes your fancy – use it!'

Charms are available depicting many hobbies, interests and nationalities, and as souvenirs from places you've visited and wish to remember.

Tassels are available to buy in several sizes small enough to use in these projects. We also like to make them from thread and beads already incorporated in the work.

Stitch-on or iron-on motifs are available at craft and haberdashery stores. They are particularly great on pieces for children as quite a large range of juvenile motifs is available.

Fringing, of the type used on cowboy outfits or dancers' costumes, can be worked quite successfully into crazy patchwork projects.

PIECING THE BASE CLOTH

Having decided on the fabrics you want to use, the next step is to piece the base cloth. There are several methods you can use, and the one you choose will be dependent to some extent on the type of project and its size.

RANDOM BLOCK

This is good for projects where any part is more than about 30 cm (12 in) square, and is quick and easy for beginners. It is not really suitable for fabrics that wriggle out of shape, like crepes or knits, unless they are interfaced. This method was used for the ruffled cushion.

1 Trace the pattern (if given) and cut two paper templates. If a pattern is not given, cut the piece(s) according to the dimensions given.

2 Depending on the size, rule three, four or five lines on one template, dividing it into sections, and mark these with a felt pen (Fig. 1).

3 Divide these larger sections into smaller sections, making sure that you have no points where four lines meet. Aim for T intersections (Fig. 2).

4 Determine the stitching order and label the parts A1, A2, A3, B1, B2, B3 and so on (Fig. 3).

5 Now, bring out your chosen fabrics and play around till you are happy with the combinations, remembering that you shouldn't place a pattern next to a pattern (Fig. 4). Note which fabric is to be cut from each small template.

6 Trace a copy of the finished design onto the second paper template, then carefully cut one of the templates along the marked lines.

7 Cut out the fabric shapes, adding a 6 mm (¼ in) seam allowance on ALL the sides.

8 On the remaining template, lay out the fabric pieces, still attached to their paper shapes. Check that your combinations are working and that you don't have two pieces of the one fabric together or two patterns.

9 Returning to the decisions you made in step 4, stitch pieces A1 and A2 together, press the seam open, then add A3. Continue with each section until you have three, four or five large irregular-shaped blocks (as shown by the felt pen lines you drew in step 2).

10 Determine the order for stitching these irregular blocks, then stitch them together until the final shape is achieved. Stitch it round the edges onto a backing cloth and, if desired, baste along the lines sewn earlier in this step to hold it in place until the embroidery is far enough advanced to keep it stable.

FIVE-SIDED CENTRE PATCH

This is good for small pieces (less than 30 cm (12 in) square. It is relatively quick, but there is greater fabric wastage than in the Random Block method. This method was used for the evening bag and the armchair caddy.

1 Cut a piece of backing fabric 5 cm (2 in) larger all round than the size needed for the project. On the wrong side, mark the cutting line and stitching lines from the pattern.

2 Select the darkest of the fabrics you plan to use and cut out a rectangle, approximately 6 cm x 8 cm (2⅜ in x 3⅛ in). Cut off one corner, making the rectangle a five-sided shape (Fig. 5).

3 Cut a rectangle of another fabric approximately 6 cm x 8 cm (2⅜ in x 3⅛ in), and pin the right sides together along the cut side of the first piece in the centre of the backing fabric (Fig. 6). Stitch the seam (through all three layers), then flip piece 2 right side up. Press the seam open.

4 Select the next piece of fabric and cut a strip 6 cm x 8 cm (2⅜ in x 3⅛ in). Pin

then stitch it in place, covering one raw end of pieces 1 and 2 (Fig. 7). Trim away any fabric behind the seam.

5 Continue to stitch on rectangles around the five-sided shape until all the edges are covered (Fig. 8). Your rectangles will increase in size as you go through each 'round'.

6 You now have a larger piece of base cloth consisting of six fabrics. Shape this into a five-sided figure (Fig. 9).

7 Begin the next round of five fabrics in the same manner as before, reshaping the base cloth into a five-sided figure after each round. Be sure to trim any excess fabric from behind the seam and press each seam open carefully.

8 When the piecing is completed, machine-stitch a row of narrow, close zigzag stitches on the cutting line marked in step 1 and hand-stitch a row of basting stitches on the stitching line.

SET PATTERN

This is similar to the Random Block method. Quick and easy, use it where two sides must be identical. This method was used for the teddy bears and the dinosaur.

1 Trace each pattern piece carefully onto white paper, making sure to label each one carefully. Mark all the lines, openings, eye and joint positions. Cut out each pattern piece (Fig. 10). Crease the pattern along each line (Fig. 11).

2 Fold the base fabric, with the right sides together. Pin all the pattern pieces to the base fabric.

3 Trace carefully round each pattern piece. Label each one, transfer the marked lines and mark a 6 mm (¼ in) seam allowance all round. Cut out each section (Fig. 12).

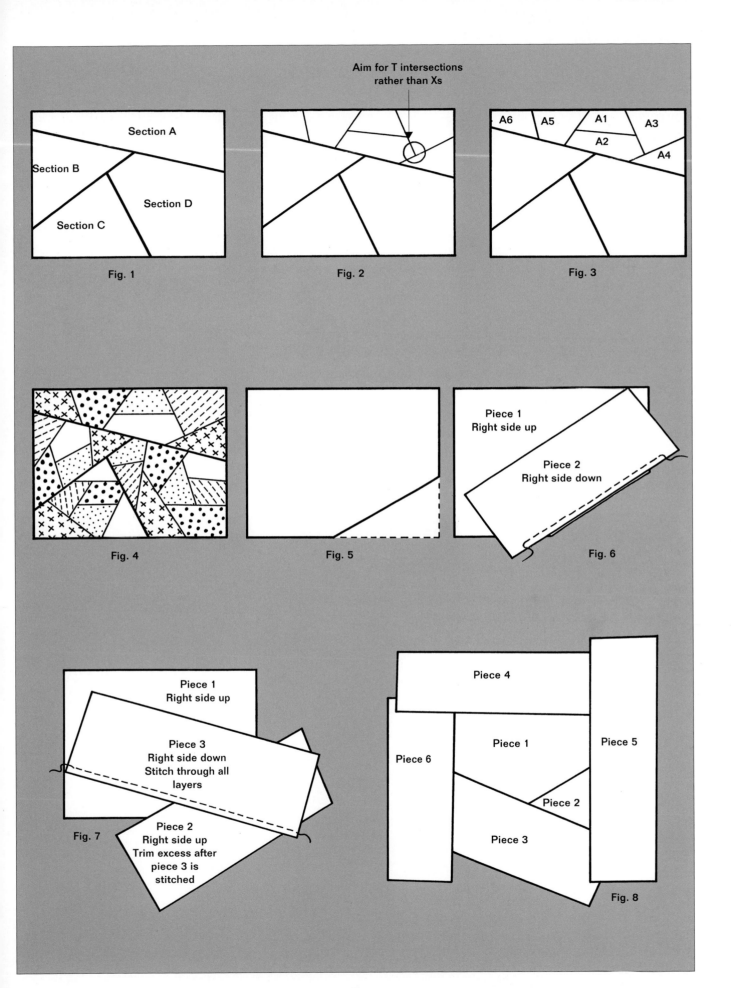

Aim for T intersections
rather than Xs

Section A

Section B

Section C

Section D

Fig. 1

Fig. 2

A6 A5 A1 A3
A2
A4

Fig. 3

Fig. 4

Fig. 5

Piece 1
Right side up

Piece 2
Right side down

Fig. 6

Piece 1
Right side up

Piece 3
Right side down
Stitch through all
layers

Piece 2
Right side up
Trim excess after
piece 3 is
stitched

Fig. 7

Piece 4

Piece 6

Piece 1

Piece 5

Piece 2

Piece 3

Fig. 8

4 While the pieces are still pinned together, mark the openings, and eye and joint positions on both sides of each piece, on the wrong side. Carefully open each part from its pair, and place them right side up on a table.

5 Transfer the marked lines to the right side of each piece of backing fabric by folding along each crease and tracing the line (don't forget that the two pieces will be mirror images of one another).

6 Cut each paper pattern piece along the marked lines. Label each section – arm 1, arm 2, arm 3 etc – (Fig. 12).

7 Using the selected fabrics and keeping them folded or doubled, with the right sides together, pin each pattern piece onto the fabric. Cut out each piece, adding a 6 mm ($^1/_4$ in) seam allowance all round. As each piece is cut, pin it into the appropriate position on the base fabric (Fig. 13).

8 Sew one part of the project at a time – for example, the inner arms, then the legs and so on. Determine the stitching order, then stitch each piece of fancy fabric to the base fabric, along the marked lines. Press each seam line before stitching the next seam. When the whole piece is patched, stitch around the edge to hold all the materials in place.

9 When the piecing is completed, machine-stitch a row of narrow, close zigzag stitches on the cutting line marked in step 1. Hand-stitch a row of basting stitches on the stitching line.

♥ RANDOM PATCHES

This is similar to the traditional Random Block method and is suitable for large or small pieces. It produces a different look to the other methods.

1 Cut the base cloth fabric 5 cm (2 in) bigger all round than the required finished size. On the wrong side, mark the cutting line and the stitching lines from the pattern.

2 Select the first two fabrics and place them on the backing fabric, with the right sides together. Stitch through all three layers of fabric, then flip the pieces open and press.

3 Add more fabric pieces (not necessarily rectangles as was required in the Centre Patch method) to either side of those sewn in step 2. Keep adding fabrics, covering all the seams you can. Those seams you can't manage with the machine can be sewn down later by hand.

4 Cut pieces to fit gaps and odd shapes and appliqué them in place, using a fine stitch in a cotton that matches the fabric.

5 Remember to trim excess fabric from behind the seams and press each as it is sewn.

6 When the piecing is completed, machine-stitch a row of narrow, close zigzag stitches on the cutting line marked in step 1. Hand-stitch a row of basting stitches on the stitching line.

♥ NARROW STRIP

This method is similar to Random Block piecing. It is quick and easy and is best used for long narrow pieces.

1 Cut the base cloth 3 cm (1$^1/_4$ in) bigger all round than the required finished size of the piece. On the wrong side, mark the cutting line and stitching lines from the pattern.

2 Select the first two fabrics and place them on the backing fabric, with the right sides together. Stitch through all three layers of fabric, then flip the pieces open and press.

3 Add another piece of fabric to cover one of the ends, forming a T intersection (Fig. 14). Repeat for the other side.

4 Keep adding fabrics at each end making sure to alter the placement angle each time (Fig. 15).

5 When the piecing is completed, machine-stitch a row of narrow, close zigzag stitches on the cutting line marked in step 1. Hand-stitch a row of basting stitches on the stitching line.

The instructions for this beautiful bear are on page 27

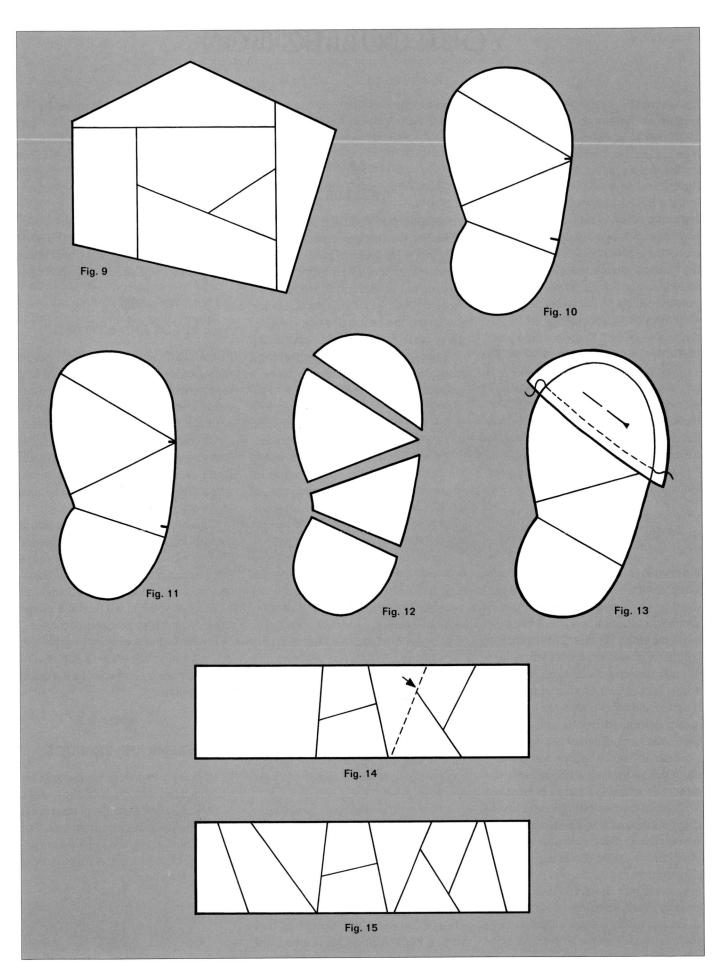

Fig. 9

Fig. 10

Fig. 11

Fig. 12

Fig. 13

Fig. 14

Fig. 15

11

BOLSTER CUSHION

A little added luxury for your bedroom or on a special chair in the lounge room, this bolster cushion is an eye-catcher.

MATERIALS

1 m (1¹⁄₈ yd) of fabric for the base cloth (also used to make the bolster insert)

Total of 55 cm x 60 cm (22 in x 24 in) of assorted fancy fabrics

20 cm x 90 cm (8 in x 36 in) of fancy fabric for the bolster ends

Two self-cover buttons, 5 cm (2 in) in diameter

20 cm x 40 cm (8 in x 16 in) of Vilene or other lightweight interfacing

40 cm (16 in) zipper to match the darkest fancy fabric

1.2 m (1¹⁄₃ yd) of piping to match the fabric for the bolster ends

Assorted embroidery threads, rayon and others

Two or three different laces or braids, totalling 1.5 m (1²⁄₃ yd)

Buttons, beads, charms etc

30 cm (12 in) each of four different colours of 3 mm (³⁄₁₆ in) wide silk ribbons

Chenille needle

Crewel needles

Straw needle or a milliner's needle for grub roses

Ordinary sewing thread

Polyester fibre fill

Drawing materials

PREPARATION

Draw a rectangle 49 cm x 54 cm (19 in x 21 in) onto the wrong side of the base cloth fabric. Cut it out, allowing an additional 3 cm (1¹⁄₄ in) all round.

CRAZY PATCHWORK

STEP ONE

Using the Random Block method, crazy patch the base fabric. On the wrong side, machine a row of zigzag stitches along the cutting line. Trim any excess fabric. Hand-sew a row of basting stitches on the stitching line.

STEP TWO

Add lace or braids to cover some of the seam lines. Cover all the remaining seam lines with your choice of embroidery stitches. Embellish these rows of stitches with beads or stitch combinations of your choice. Do not bead past the row of hand-basting.

STEP THREE

Add lace motifs, ribbon embroidery, tassels, beads and buttons to complete the decoration. Stitch a message, if desired.

MAKING UP

STEP ONE

Fold the bolster fabric with the right sides together. Stitch from **A** to the end, reinforcing the stitching at **A** with

Rosebuds in variegated rayon ribbon with silk tape leaves and stems

16

several back stitches. Stitch from **B** to the end, reinforcing at **B** with several back stitches (Fig. 1). Turn the piece right side out and insert the zipper in the opening.

STEP TWO

Beginning at the seam, pin the piping over the hand-basting. Using the zipper foot, and stitching on top of the stitching on the piping (or as close to it as possible), apply the piping right round both ends of the bolster. Overlap the ends of the piping and trim them to 1 cm (³/₈ in). Leave the ends of the piping loose on the outside.

STEP THREE

From the Vilene or other interfacing, cut two circles, each 18 cm (7 in) in diameter. Cut the fancy fabric for the ends in half lengthwise, so each piece is 10 cm x 90 cm (4 in x 36 in). Join the short ends to make a circle. Fold the circle into quarters and mark the four points. Quarter each Vilene circle and mark the points. Pin the four points on the fabric circle to the four points on the Vilene circle. Pleat the fabric evenly in a fan-like manner to fit each quarter (Fig. 2). Aim to have the pleats deeper and sitting neatly over the top of one another in the centre. Stitch the pleats in place.

STEP FOUR

Cover the buttons and stitch them into place over the centre of the pleated ends, stitching through all layers.

STEP FIVE

Open the zipper and turn the bolster to the wrong side. Placing the fabrics with the right sides together, fit the pleated circles into the ends of the bolster. Using the zipper foot, stitch exactly over the piping stitching. Clip the curves, press the seams open carefully and turn the bolster to the right side.

STEP SIX

For the bolster insert, cut a 53 cm (21 in) square and two circles 18 cm (7 in) in diameter from the remaining base cloth fabric. Stitch the square to form a tube, leaving a 20 cm (8 in) opening in the seam. Insert the circles in the ends. Clip the curves, press the seams open and turn the insert right side out. Fill the insert with the polyester fill and slipstitch the opening closed. Insert the bolster into the cover and close the zipper.

Lavender sprigs in silk ribbon with pearl cotton branches

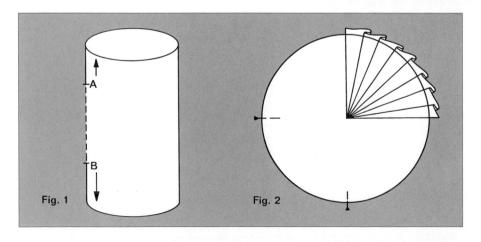

Fig. 1

Fig. 2

MEMORIES BOX

Everyone has a collection of family treasures – the baby's first dress or booties, a favourite childhood book, letters, cards and photos. Make this beautiful box to keep them safe.

MATERIALS

25 cm x 35 cm (10 in x 14 in) card-board or papier-mâché box

30 cm (12 in) of plain fabric (to cover the box sides and use as one of the plain fabrics on the top)

25 cm x 35 cm (10 in x 14 in) of cream felt

30 cm x 40 cm (12 in x 15 in) of fabric for the base cloth

Fabric for lining the box (optional)

Scraps of six or seven fancy fabrics

50 cm (20 in) of cotton lace

Rayon thread, Cream

Embroidery threads

Braids

Silk ribbons

Assorted buttons, charms and beads

Crewel needles

Chenille needles

Beading needles

Ordinary sewing thread, Cream

1.5 m (1²/₃ yd) of antique-look gold braid

25 cm x 35 cm (10 in x 14 in) of wadding

Spray adhesive

Hot glue gun

Tacky glue

Pencil

Tracing or tissue paper

Pegs

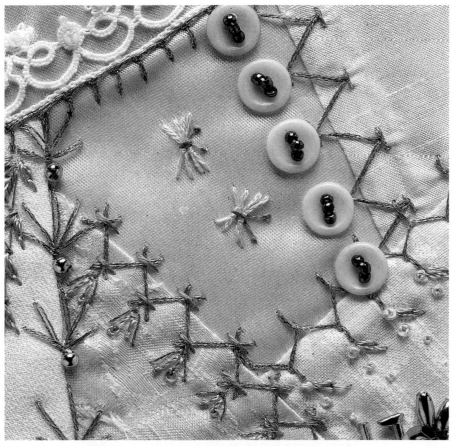

Mother of pearl buttons with beads and dainty butterflies

PREPARATION

STEP ONE

Measure around the box lid and add 2 cm (³/₄ in). Cut a strip of plain fabric this measurement long and 2.5 cm (1 in) wide. Set it aside. Measure the distance around the four sides of the box and add 2 cm (³/₄ in). Measure the depth of the box and add 4 cm (1³/₄ in). Cut a rectangle with these measurements and set it aside.

STEP TWO

Trace the outline of the lid onto the wrong side of the base cloth fabric. Mark a second line 1.5 cm (⁵/₈ in) outside the first line. Cut out, allowing an additional 3 cm (1¹/₄ in) all round.

CRAZY PATCHWORK

STEP ONE

On the right side of the base cloth, and using the Centre Patch method, cover the base cloth with fancy fabrics. Include the remainder of the fabric used for the box sides.

STEP TWO

Once the base cloth is pieced, turn it over and machine a line of stitching on the outer line drawn previously. Hand-sew a row of basting stitches on the inner line.

STEP THREE

Add lace and braid to cover some of the seams. Cover all the remaining seams with your choice of embroidery stitches. Embellish these rows of stitches with beads or stitch combinations. Do not bead outside the basting line. Fill the plain spaces with embroidery, beads, buttons, charms and lace motifs, as desired. Sign and date your work, if you wish.

MAKING UP

STEP ONE

Check that the line of basting stitches matches the edge of the lid. Adjust it, if necessary. Using a fine machine zigzag stitch, sew over the row of machine-stitching made earlier. Carefully trim away all the excess material.

STEP TWO

Fold under 5 mm (¹/₄ in) on the narrow end of the first long strip cut and set aside. Apply tacky glue carefully around the edge of the lid and position the fabric so it can be folded over the edge and up inside the lid. Allow the glue to dry. Apply tacky glue to the inside of the lid sides and fold the fabric up and inside onto the glue. Use pegs to hold the fabric in place while the glue dries.

STEP THREE

Apply tacky glue to the top of the lid. Work quickly and spread the glue evenly. Place the wadding on top of the glue and press down firmly to ensure contact. Allow to dry, then trim the excess wadding, using sharp scissors.

STEP FOUR

Place the patchwork over the wadding and ensure that the overhang is even on all sides. Fold the overhang down to check that it comes about halfway down the side of the lid. If it is too big, sew another line of zigzag stitches at the correct distance and trim away the excess patchwork.

STEP FIVE

Using the glue gun, carefully glue the centre point of the raw short end to the lid. Repeat for the other end, then for the centre points of the long sides. Stretch the fabric slightly each time to give a wrinkle-free top. Repeat until the piece is stretched and glued in place all round.

STEP SIX

Using the glue gun, carefully glue the braid around the outside of the lid to hide the edge of the patchwork piece.

STEP SEVEN

To cover the outside of the box, fold under 1 cm (³/₈ in) on one short end of the remaining piece of fabric. Glue it carefully to the centre of the box side at the back so 2 cm (³/₄ in) extends above the rim. Apply glue sparingly to the box, then glue the fabric into place. Fold the top allowance to the inside and stick it down. At the bottom, carefully clip the fabric at the four corners, then neatly glue the bottom allowance to the box. Glue the piece of felt to the bottom of the box, using only as much glue as is necessary to hold it.

Single rose stitched in cream silk ribbon with metallic thread centre

20

CHILD'S VEST

This sweet little vest was made for the granddaughter of a friend. It is a simple one-piece pattern and is reversible – although it has never been worn with the crazy patchwork side inside!

To fit: 8–10 year old

MATERIALS

Tissue paper
50 cm (20 in) of fabric for the base cloth
50 cm (20 in) of lightweight denim
Total of 60 cm (24 in) of fancy fabrics
Embroidery threads
Assorted beads, buttons, ribbon, laces and lace motifs
Crewel needle
Ordinary sewing thread
2 m (2¼ yd) of black satin bias binding
Front closure (optional)
Tracing paper and pencil

PREPARATION

See the vest pattern on the Pull Out Pattern Sheet.

STEP ONE

Trace the pattern onto the tissue paper and cut it out.

STEP TWO

Pin the pattern to the base cloth fabric. Transfer the cutting line and the stitching lines onto the wrong side of the fabric. Cut out, allowing an additional 2 cm (¾ in) all round.

CRAZY PATCHWORK

STEP ONE

Work with the right side of the base cloth fabric facing up and the lines drawn on the underside. Using the Random Block method, crazy patch the vest pieces.

STEP TWO

On the wrong side, stitch a row of machine-stitching on the cutting line and hand-sew a line of basting on the stitching line.

EMBELLISHING

STEP ONE

Cover all the seams with your choice of embroidery stitches. Embellish these rows of stitches with beads and/or stitch combinations. Do not bead outside the basting lines.

STEP TWO

Fill the plain fabric patches with additional embroidery in either silk or cotton thread or a combination. Add beads, buttons, charms, lace motifs and so on.

Back view

STEP THREE

Sign and date your work in an unobtrusive place.

MAKING UP

STEP ONE

Cut the lining from the lightweight denim. Place the vest and the lining together with the right sides facing. Pin, then stitch the armholes. Note that the shoulder seams have not yet been joined. Clip the curves, press and turn the vest to the right side.

STEP TWO

Open the vest and the lining at the shoulder. Place them right sides together and stitch from the neck edge of the lining across to the neck edge of the vest, matching the seams exactly. Press and refold the vest to form the shoulders.

STEP THREE

Check the alignment of the vest and lining, which are stitched together at the shoulder seam but not joined together elsewhere. Baste the vest and the lining together. Starting at the centre of the lower back, pin bias binding along the back, up the front edge, round the neck, down the other front and return to the centre back. Using the zipper foot, stitch the binding in place. Stitch on the fold of the bias binding and align it exactly with the row of hand-basting already in place. Slipstitch the other side of the bias binding to the lining. Add a closure at the front, if desired.

WOOL QUILT

This bed quilt is made from woollen fabrics in rich, warm tones. Add a
wadding layer if you prefer a warmer quilt.

MATERIALS

3.2 m (3¹/₂ yd) of 240 cm (94 in) wide
calico for the base cloth and the
backing

1 m (1¹/₈ yd) of red velvet or velveteen for the sashes and border or
1.8 m (2 yd) if you prefer not to
have joins

Total of 1.5 m (1²/₃ yd) of scraps of
woollen fabrics

Wadding (optional)

Ordinary sewing thread

Tapestry wool or 8-ply knitting wool,
Blue

Assorted other woollen threads

Chenille needle

7 m (7³/₄ yd) of black satin bias
binding

Several packets of small safety pins

CRAZY PATCHWORK

STEP ONE

From the base cloth fabric, cut twelve
31 cm (12¹/₂ in) squares. Using the
Centre Patch method or any combination of methods, crazy patch the twelve
blocks. On each block, machine a row
of zigzag stitches along the cutting line,
trim any excess fabric. Hand-sew a
row of basting on the stitching line.

STEP TWO

Using woollen threads, cover all the
seam lines with your choice of embroidery stitches. Embellish these rows of
stitches with stitch combinations.

MAKING UP

STEP ONE

From the calico, cut the backing fabric
to measure 140 cm x 180 cm (55¹/₈ in x
71 in). Place a clean sheet on the floor
(few people have a table big enough
for the next steps). Lay the backing
fabric on the sheet and position the
crazy squares on it, following the
placement diagram.

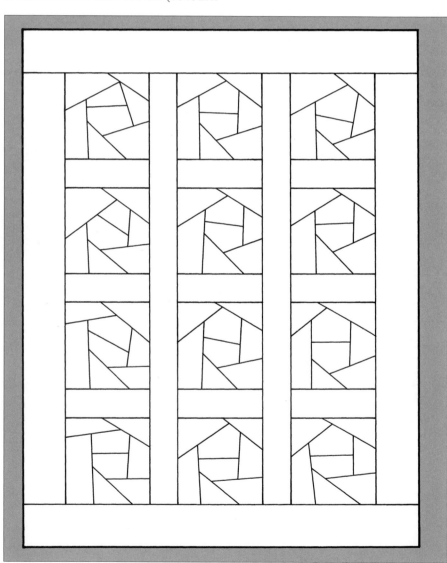

Quilt Placement Diagram

STEP TWO

From the red velvet, cut the following pieces:
- nine strips, each 8 cm x 31 cm (3 in x 12½ in);
- two strips, each 8 cm x 150 cm (3 in x 60 in);
- two strips, each 15 cm x 105 cm (6 in x 42 in); and
- two strips, each 15 cm x 180 cm (6 in x 72 in).

For the longer strips, you will have to join lengths.

STEP THREE

Following the placement diagram on page 24, stitch the blocks and the nine small strips into three long rows. Join the rows with a 150 cm (60 in) strip in between each pair.

STEP FOUR

Add the top borders, then the two side borders to the quilt top.

STEP FIVE

Lay the completed quilt top right side up on the calico backing, inserting a wadding layer, if desired. Make sure it is smooth and completely wrinkle-free. Beginning in the middle, pin the layers together, using the safety pins.

STEP SIX

Using the blue tapestry wool, feather stitch around each block. This does the double duty of holding the quilt layers together and decorating the seam lines at the same time.

STEP SEVEN

Stitch, by hand or machine, a row of stitches close to the edge of the quilt top to hold the edges together. Trim any excess backing fabric. Unfold the satin bias binding and, using the fold line as a stitching guide, stitch the binding to the front of the quilt with the right sides together. Slipstitch the other side of the bias binding neatly to the back of the quilt.

Wool daisies and forget-me-nots

Blackberries and briar roses in variegated crochet cotton

TEDDY BEAR

Popular among crazy patchworkers and bear enthusiasts alike, this little fellow will sit happily wherever you put him.

Note: This bear is not a toy. Do not give it to small children to play with.

MATERIALS

Tracing paper
Pencil
Ruler
60 cm (24 in) of poplin or sheeting for the base cloth
Total of approximately 80 cm (32 in) of a variety of coordinating fabrics
Approximately 50 cm (20 in) of two or three different laces
Ordinary sewing thread
Stranded cotton or Perle cotton in the main colour
Assorted embroidery threads to tone or contrast
Assorted beads, buttons, charms etc
Silk ribbon
Braid
Crewel needles
Beading needles
Chenille needles
Curved needle
Polyester fibre fill
Set of bear joints, 40 mm (1^1/$_3$ in) in diameter, or four buttons
Dental floss
Growler (optional)
Safety eyes, 15 mm (^{5}/$_8$ in) or 18 mm (^{3}/$_4$ in)
80 cm (32 in) of 20 mm (^{3}/$_4$ in) wide satin ribbon for the neck bow
Thick cardboard or plastic, such as an ice-cream container
Craft glue

CRAZY PATCHWORK

See the pattern on the Pull Out Pattern Sheet.

STEP ONE

Using the pattern and the Set Pattern method, transfer all the pattern details. Cut out and crazy patch all the pieces. Once the base cloth is pieced, turn it over and machine a line of stitching on the outer line. Hand-sew a row of basting stitches on the inner line.

STEP TWO

Add lace and/or braid to cover some of the seams. Cover all the remaining seams with your choice of embroidery stitches. Embellish these rows of stitches with beads and stitch combinations, making sure not to bead outside the basting line.

STEP THREE

Fill the spaces on the plain patches with embroidery, beads, buttons, charms or lace motifs. Stitch a message or the name of the bear, if it is to be a gift. Sign and date your bear.

MAKING UP

STEP ONE

With the right sides together and using a 6 mm (^{1}/$_4$ in) seam allowance for all seams, pin together both arms. Using a small stitch length, stitch the arms together, leaving an opening as marked on the pattern.

A blue button flower with sequin leaves and beads

Back view with 'love, luck and laughter' stitched on one side

Left view showing the embroidery on the shoulder and paw

Pin and stitch together both legs from toe to heel.

STEP THREE

Pin and stitch two fronts together and two backs together. Align the centre back and centre front seams at the bear's bottom, then stitch the side seams from neck edge to neck edge.

STEP FOUR

Pin and stitch the two side heads together from the nose to the neck. Fold the head gusset in half lengthwise to determine the exact centre point of the nose. Matching the centre point of the gusset EXACTLY with the centre front head seam, pin and stitch from the centre to the bottom of the neck on one side of the head. Check the alignment, then repeat for the other side.

STEP FIVE

Pin and stitch the ears together.

STEP SIX

Trim any fabric that is outside the 6 mm ($^{1}/_{4}$ in) seam allowance. Clip the curves and turn all the pieces to the right side. You should now have: one head (open at the neck edge), one body (open at the neck edge), two arms (open for about 6 cm ($2^{3}/_{8}$ in) along the back seam), two legs (open at the foot), two ears (open along the bottom edges), and two foot pads.

STEP SEVEN

Insert one part of each joint into each arm, placing the joint at the position marked. Repeat for the legs. Take care with this step to ensure you have a right and a left of each limb.

STEP EIGHT

Fill the arms first. The secret of a good bear is not to try and put the filling into each section in one go. At first, use pieces of filling about the size of a cotton wool ball. Tease each small piece of filling and prod it down to the ends with a chopstick or wooden spoon handle. You will be surprised at just how much stuffing is needed – just when you think it is full enough, give it a good poke and add some more. Make sure that the arms are all of equal fullness and hardness, then stitch the opening closed, using small ladder stitches.

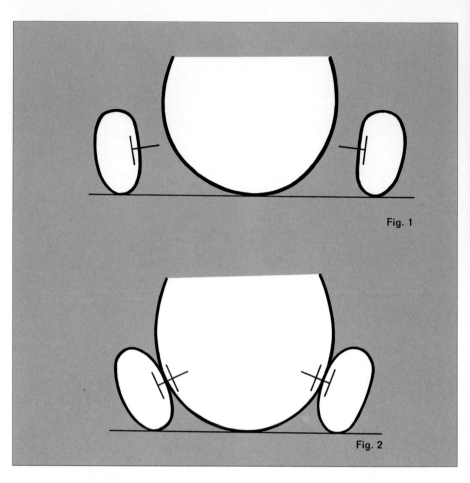

Fig. 1

Fig. 2

STEP NINE

Fill the legs as far as you can. Turn up the seam allowance on the bottom of the leg and baste it in place. Cut a piece of cardboard or plastic slightly smaller than the paper foot pad pattern. Glue a little filling onto one side of the cardboard or plastic, then carefully position the foot pad on top. Glue the seam allowance of the foot pad around the underside of the cardboard or plastic. Matching the heel and toe seams and the two appropriate points on the foot pad, sew several stitches to hold the foot pad in place. Use basting stitches to ease the leg and the foot pad to a good fit. Stitch half the foot pad to the leg using very small stitches, but make sure to catch both layers of material. Continue adding filling until the legs are the same fullness as the arms, then finish the seam on the foot pad.

STEP TEN

Start to fill the body and, when it is about one-third full, attach the legs. Begin by sitting the body on a table and holding the legs next to where you think they should attach. The end of the joint will poke out of the leg. With the bottom and the lower side of both legs flat on the table, mark the place where the joint ends touch the sides of the body (it will be somewhere close to where the mark is on the inside of the front). Sometimes it is easier to have a friend mark this position (Fig. 1). Following the instructions for the type of joint you are using, attach the legs to the body and tighten the joints hard. Add more filling around the joint ends.

STEP ELEVEN

If you are using a growler, wrap it in some filling or a piece of wadding and place it in the body now. Continue

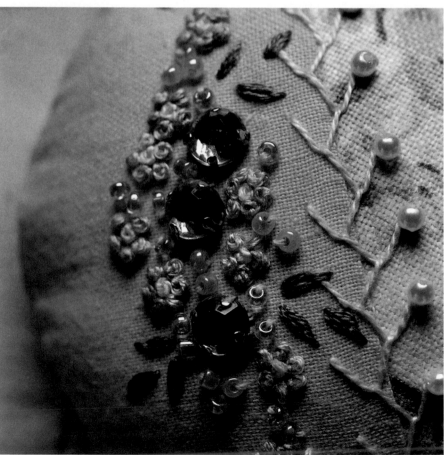

French knot forget-me-nots, stitch-on 'jewels' and seed beads

adding the filling until you are up to where the arm positions are marked. Attach the arms at the points marked and again tighten the joints hard.

STEP TWELVE

Continue to add filling until it keeps falling out of the neck hole. Turn under the seam allowance on the neck edges of both the head and the body. Baste it in place with a double length of thread, leaving enough thread at each end to hold easily. This thread will be used to gather the head or neck edges slightly to ensure a perfect fit.

STEP THIRTEEN

Attach the safety eyes in the positions indicated, making very sure they are even and equally placed. Nothing looks sillier than a cross-eyed bear.

STEP FOURTEEN

Fill the head, paying particular attention to the nose. It must be very firm so the stitching looks good on the finished bear. When you can't add any more filling to the head, align the centre front seams of the head and the body and sew a few stitches to hold them. Line up the dart seams on the head with the body side seams and sew a few stitches to hold. Use the seam allowance holding row to ease the head and body to fit. Thread the curved needle with 60 cm (24 in) of dental floss and make a double knot 7 cm (2³/₄ in) from the end. Using the dental floss and sewing a back stitch through the fabric over the knot to secure it, stitch the head to the body from the neck dart/side seam holding stitches across the back to the other neck dart. Do not cut the dental floss.

STEP FIFTEEN

Continue to add filling, poking it up into the head and down into the body. It must be very firm or the head will wobble. Stitch to the centre front seam and add more filling. When you can't add any more, complete the seam. To finish, stitch a knot, thread the starting end of the dental floss onto the needle and take the needle (carrying two threads) through the neck to the back, pull hard, then cut it close to the fabric.

The end of the dental floss should pop back into the body and never come undone. Remove all the basting threads.

STEP SIXTEEN

Fill the ears. Turn up the seam allowance on the bottom edges of the ears and slipstitch them together. Decide on the ear positions and pin the ears in place. Stand back and make sure you're happy with the position – ear placement can change the whole personality of a bear. Stitch the ears in place, making sure they are level with each other and an equal distance from the eyes.

STEP SEVENTEEN

Using six strands of embroidery cotton, embroider the nose and mouth. Turn the ends of the mouth up, down or straight out sideways, depending on your bear's personality.

STEP EIGHTEEN

Using the wide satin ribbon, tie a bow around the bear's neck.

Silk ribbon fuchsias

Pink silk ribbon roses with blue pistil-stitch flowers

EVENING JACKET

A timeless fashion accessory, this beautiful jacket is sure
to become a favourite piece in your wardrobe.

BEFORE YOU BEGIN

I used a commercial pattern. Select a
simple style without darts.

Check the yardage requirement for
your pattern; that will be the requirement for the base cloth fabric. You will
need a total of 3 m (3³/₄ yd) more of
fancy fabrics. Select six to eight fabrics
and divide the requirement by that
number to determine the amount of
each fabric required.

Check the pattern for the quantity of
lining fabric required. I prefer poplin
because it doesn't slither about like
synthetic lining fabric.

MATERIALS

Tissue paper and pencil
Commercial pattern
Fabric for the base cloth
Fancy fabrics
Poplin for the lining
Stranded cotton: Burgundy, Cream,
    Pink, Green
Assorted embroidery threads to
    match or contrast
Metallic embroidery thread, Silver
Assorted silk ribbons to match or
    contrast
Assorted beads, three to five
    different kinds
Buttons, charms, lace motifs, sequins
1 m (1¹/₈ yd) each of two or three
    different cotton laces
2 m (2¹/₄ yd) of 10 cm (4 in) wide
    satin ribbon: two, three or four
    colours
Sewing thread to match the lining
Crewel needles
Beading needles
Chenille needles

PREPARATION

STEP ONE

Trace and cut out the required pieces
from the commercial pattern onto tissue paper.

STEP TWO

Pin the pattern pieces onto the base
cloth fabric and transfer the cutting line
and stitching lines onto the wrong
sides of the fabric. Cut out, allowing an
additional 2 cm (³/₄ in) all round. Transfer all the pattern lines and markings
onto all the pattern pieces.

CRAZY PATCHWORK

STEP ONE

Work with the right side of the base
cloth fabric facing up and the marked
lines on the underside. Using the Random Block method or the Random
Patch method, or a combination of
both, crazy patch all the pieces required for the jacket.

STEP TWO

On the wrong side, stitch a row of
machine-stitching on the cutting line
and hand-sew a line of basting on the
stitching lines.

Frog and mouse

Purple and pink sprig flowers

Teddy bear button among the roses

EMBELLISHING

STEP ONE

Apply lace to some seam lines, trying to achieve roughly the same number of lace pieces on both fronts and on both sleeves.

STEP TWO

Cover all the remaining seams with your choice of embroidery stitches. Embellish these rows of stitches with beads and/or stitch combinations. Do not bead outside the basting lines. For comfortable wearing, do not bead the middle to lower back, the area of the sleeves that could be rested on a table, or under the arms (arm or jacket body).

STEP THREE

Fill the plain fabric patches with additional embroidery in either silk or cotton thread or a combination of both. Add beads, buttons, charms, lace motifs, sequins and so on.

STEP FOUR

Sign and date your work in an unobtrusive place.

STEP FIVE

Using a fine machine zigzag, stitch over the row of machine stitches made in step 2 of Crazy Patchwork. Cut away the excess fabric carefully.

MAKING UP

Complete the jacket, following the pattern instructions. Topstitch 6 mm (¹/₄ in) from the edges, taking extreme care near beads, buttons or sequins.

Note: When making up the jacket, some seams will need to be pressed open. Do this over a thick towel folded to provide padding for the embroidery stitches so they will not be flattened.

Back view of the evening jacket

ALBUM COVER

This album cover was designed as a wedding gift, but you could just as easily make one in pastel pinks or blues as a christening gift, or in stronger colours for a twenty-first birthday.

MATERIALS

Refillable photo album
White paper
Ruler
50 cm (18 in) square of fabric for the base cloth
Total of approximately 60 cm (24 in) square of fancy fabrics
1 m (1¹⁄₈ yd) of cream satin for the lining and back cover
40 cm (15 in) of wadding
Embroidery thread: Cream, Gold, Pale Green
Assorted gold and cream beads
Cream sequins
Different laces and braids totalling 70 cm (28 in)
Lace motifs or panels
7 mm (⁵⁄₁₆ in) wide silk ribbon, Cream
50 cm (18 in) of 7 mm (⁵⁄₁₆ in) wide ribbon, Gold
Heart-shaped buttons
Tassels
Ordinary sewing thread, White
Crewel needle
Chenille needle
Beading needle
Craft glue
Pegs

PREPARATION

Dismantle the album and measure the front cover. The patchwork piece covers only the front cover. Exact measurements are crucial here.

CRAZY PATCHWORK

STEP ONE

Using the Random Block or Centre Patch method, crazy patch the base fabric for the front cover piece.

STEP TWO

Add lace or braids to cover some of the seam lines. Cover all the remaining seam lines with your choice of embroidery stitches. Embellish these rows of stitches with beads or stitch combinations of your choice.

STEP THREE

Add lace motifs, ribbon embroidery, tassels, beads and buttons to complete the decoration. Stitch a message, if desired.

MAKING UP

STEP ONE

Spread craft glue evenly all over the front cover and lay the piece of wadding over the glued surface. Allow the glue to dry, then carefully trim away any excess wadding.

Tubular braid stitched down with gold beads and gold thread

35

STEP TWO

Cut a strip of satin 7 cm (2³/₄ in) wide by the album width plus 2 cm (³/₄ in) and sew it to the crazy patchwork top (Fig. 1).

STEP THREE

Cut three pieces each as wide as the album plus 2 cm (³/₄ in) by the album length plus 8 cm (3¹/₈ in) (Fig. 2). Stitch two of these pieces together with a bare 1 cm (³/₈ in) seam allowance to form a bag that the back cover will slide into. Stitch the remaining piece to the crazy patchwork top with a bare 1 cm (³/₈ in) seam allowance, forming the front cover sleeve. Carefully slide the covers into the sleeves and check that the fit is tight but not straining the seams. Adjust the seams, if necessary.

STEP FOUR

Opening out the part of the cover that folds over to conceal the screws, place the back cover in its sleeve (outside down) on a table. Pull the fabric taut and glue the outside seam allowance over the edge and onto the inside. Secure it with pegs, if necessary, until it is dry. Trim any excess. Pull the fabric taut on the inside of the cover and fold the seam allowance to the inside. Trim any excess and use pegs to hold it in position. Stitch the ends together, making sure that you maintain the tension on the fabric so the cover will be taut and smooth when finished. Repeat for the front cover but lay it on a towel so the embroidery is not flattened.

STEP FIVE

Reassemble the album, using the 1 cm (³/₈ in) ribbon to hold the pages in place, or punch holes and add hole-reinforcing rings to accommodate the post-style hinges.

Use metallic thread to stitch a message

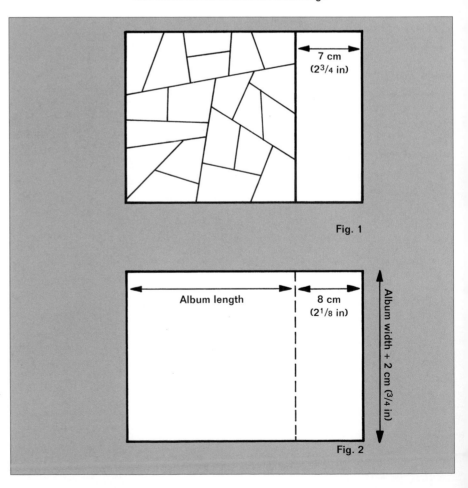

HAT BOX

Hat boxes do not have to be used only for storing hats. They are equally wonderful for keeping embroidery or other sewing in. This particular hat box belongs to my sister and is made in some of her favourite colours.

MATERIALS

35 cm (14 in) diameter hat box
40 cm (15 in) of plain fabric (to cover the box sides and use as one of the plain fabrics on the top)
40 cm (16 in) square of fabric for the base cloth
35 cm (14 in) diameter circle of felt
Scraps of six or seven fancy fabrics
50 cm (20 in) of cotton lace
Braids, lace, charms etc
Stranded cotton, Cream
Embroidery threads
Silk ribbons
Assorted buttons and beads
Crewel needles
Chenille needles
Beading needles
Ordinary sewing thread: White, Grey/mauve
Tasselled braid to fit around the lid
35 cm (14 in) square of wadding
Spray adhesive
Hot glue gun
Tacky glue
Pencil
Pegs

PREPARATION

STEP ONE

Measure the circumference of the box and the depth of the box side. From the plain fabric, cut a strip 3 cm (1¼ in) wide by the circumference plus 2 cm (¾ in). Cut another piece the size of the depth plus 5 cm (2 in) by the circumference plus 2 cm (¾ in). Set them aside.

STEP TWO

Trace the outline of the box lid onto the wrong side of the base cloth fabric. Mark a second line, 1.5 cm (⅝ in) outside the outline.

CRAZY PATCHWORK

STEP ONE

On the right side of the base cloth and using the Centre Patch method, cover the base cloth with fancy fabrics. Include the remainder of the fabric used for the box side as one of your fabrics.

STEP TWO

Once the base cloth is pieced, turn it over and machine a line of stitching on the outer line. Hand-baste a row of stitches on the inner line.

STEP THREE

Add lace and/or braid to cover some of the seams. Cover all the remaining seams with your choice of embroidery stitches. Embellish these rows of stitches with beads or stitch combinations. Do not bead outside the basting line. Fill the spaces on the plain patches with embroidery, beads, buttons, charms and lace motifs.

STEP FOUR

Sign and date your work, if desired.

MAKING UP

STEP ONE

Using a fine machine zigzag stitch, sew over the row of machine-stitching made earlier. Trim away all excess fabric carefully.

STEP TWO

Turn under and press a 1 cm (⅜ in) seam allowance at one end of both pieces of plain fabric already cut. The narrower piece will edge the lid. Apply tacky glue carefully around the edge of the lid and position the fabric so it can be folded over the edge and up inside the lid. Allow the glue to dry. Apply tacky glue to the inside edge of the lid, then fold the fabric up and inside. Use pegs to hold the fabric in place while the glue dries.

STEP THREE

Using the spray adhesive, apply the larger piece of plain fabric to the outside of the box. Allow 2 cm (¾ in) to fold over and inside the box and 3 cm (1¼ in) to fold over onto the base.

STEP FOUR

Apply tacky glue to the top of the lid. Work quickly and spread the glue evenly. Place the piece of wadding on top of the glue. Press it down firmly to ensure good contact and allow the glue to dry. Using sharp scissors, trim away the excess wadding.

STEP FIVE

Place the crazy patchwork piece over the wadding and ensure that the overhang is even on all sides. Fold the overhang down to check that it comes about halfway down the side of the lid. If the piece is too big, sew another line of zigzag stitching inside the first one and trim away the excess.

STEP SIX

Place pins in the patchwork at the clock face points of twelve, three, six and nine. Using the glue gun, stick points twelve and six to the lid, stretching the fabric to eliminate wrinkles. Repeat for points three and nine, stretching the fabric as before. Repeat for points one, seven, four and ten, then all around until the entire piece is stretched and glued in place.

STEP SEVEN

Using the glue gun, carefully glue the border of tasselled braid around the edge of the lid, covering the edge of the patchwork.

STEP EIGHT

Cut a piece of felt slightly smaller than the base and glue it in position on the base. Line the box, if and as desired.

Silver buttons are used as flowers in this delicate spray

SEWING BOX

This exquisite little sewing box, with its fold-down sides, holds all
your sewing essentials.

MATERIALS

White paper
Ruler
Pencil
Tailor's chalk
14 cm (5½ in) square fabric for the
   base cloth
50 cm (20 in) square of thick
   cardboard
30 cm x 40 cm (12 in x 16 in) of thin
   cardboard (a cereal box is ideal)
50 cm x 58 cm (20 in x 23 in) of plain
   fabric to cover the box
50 cm x 58 cm (20 in x 23 in) of fancy
   fabric for the lining
30 cm x 40 cm (12 in x 16 in) of thin
   wadding or Pellon
1 m (1⅛ yd) of 1 cm (⅜ in) wide
   ribbon
Ordinary sewing thread
Total of 25 cm (10 in) square of fancy
   fabrics
Quick-drying craft glue
Assorted beads, buttons, charms etc
Rayon embroidery thread, in colours
   to match and contrast with the
   fabrics
Embroidery threads to contrast with
   and match the fabrics
50 cm (20 in) of 3 mm (³⁄₁₆ in) wide
   silk ribbon
Small piece of fine grade sandpaper
Pegs

PREPARATION

Note: Do not cut out the main fabric
pieces at this stage. All the fabric is cut
adding a 1 cm (⅜ in) allowance on all
sides. Cut the ribbon adding a 1 cm
(⅜ in) allowance to each end.

   Mark the name on each cardboard
piece as you cut it out and lightly sand
all the cut edges with fine sandpaper.

   Draw up the following pieces:

- Four pieces, 10.5 cm x 12 cm (4⅛ in
x 4¾ in) each, from the thick cardboard and from the main fabric for the
box sides;
- Four pieces, 5 cm x 10 cm (2 in x
4 in) each, from the thick cardboard

and from the main fabric for the inner
box sides;

- Four pieces, 10 cm x 11.5 cm (4 in x
4½ in) each, from the thin cardboard,
the wadding and the contrasting fabric
for the box side linings;
- Four pieces, 5 cm x 10 cm (2 in x
4 in) each, from the thin cardboard, the
wadding, the contrasting fabric for the
inner box lining;
- One 11 cm (4¼ in) square each
from the thick cardboard and from the
main fabric for the box base;
- One 11.5 cm (4½ in) square each
from the thick cardboard and from the
base cloth fabric for the box lid (crazy
patch frame);
- One 10.5 cm (4⅛ in) square each
from the thin cardboard and from the

The sewing box opens to reveal a collection of accessories

41

contrasting fabric for the base lining;
• One 11 cm (4¼ in) square each from the thin cardboard and the main fabric for the lid lining;
• Four pieces of 1 cm (³/₈ in) wide ribbon, 13 cm (5 in) long;
• Four pieces of 1 cm (³/₈ in) wide ribbon, 8 cm (3¼ in) long.

CRAZY PATCHWORK

STEP ONE

Using the Centre Patch method, crazy patch the base cloth for the lid, using the fancy fabrics. On the wrong side, machine a row of zigzag stitches along the cutting line, trim any excess fabric. Hand-sew a row of basting on the stitching line.

STEP TWO

Cover all the seams with your choice of embroidery stitches, using the rayon thread. Embellish these rows of stitches with beads or stitch combinations. Do not bead outside the basting line. Add lace motifs, ribbon embroidery, tassels, beads and buttons.

MAKING UP

STEP ONE

Glue wadding to one side of the cardboard marked 'crazy patch frame'. Trim the excess. Place the completed crazy patchwork piece right side down on a clean surface with the padded cardboard (wadding side to the wrong side of the patchwork) on top. Carefully glue the seam allowances of the patchwork piece to the wrong side of the cardboard, stretching it slightly to ensure a firm fit. Use pegs to hold it until the glue dries.

STEP TWO

On the main fabric pieces for the box sides, mark the embroidery area with tailor's chalk (Fig. 1). Complete the embroidery before cutting out. See the stitch samplers on pages 13-15 for

Pink and gold tassels

Folded satin ribbon flowers and embroidered baby's breath

42

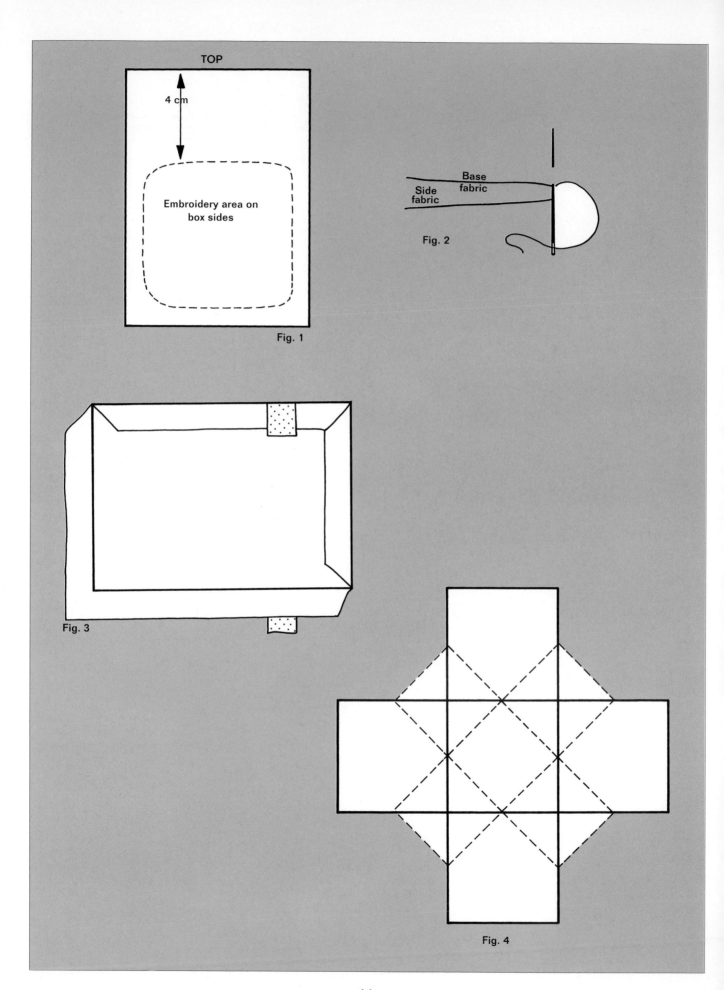

TOP

4 cm

Embroidery area on
box sides

Fig. 1

Side
fabric

Base
fabric

Fig. 2

Fig. 3

Fig. 4

44

embroidery ideas. Glue the embroidered fabric to the corresponding thick cardboard pieces, making sure the glue goes only onto the seam allowances. Stretch each piece slightly as you glue it, to get a firm fit. Use pegs to hold the fabric in place while the glue dries.

STEP THREE

Cover the base cardboard with the main fabric. With the right sides together and using a doubled thread, stitch the box sides to the base (Fig. 2).

STEP FOUR

For the linings of the box sides, glue wadding to the thin cardboard, then cover it with the fancy fabric. Attach the ribbon 3 cm (1¼ in) from the top. Be sure that ribbon is only glued to the back on the seam allowances (Fig. 3). Glue the linings to the box sides.

STEP FIVE

Make the base lining, then fit and glue it in place.

STEP SIX

Construct the inner box, following steps 2–5 above, omitting the embroidery, and set it aside.

STEP SEVEN

Following the pattern, cut, then cover, the thick cardboard piece that forms the thimble box. Fold, then glue the seam allowances under, then glue them to the inside of the box. Fold up the sides to form the box and blind stitch to hold them in place.

STEP EIGHT

Cut the lining cardboard and fabric for the thimble box base. Glue the fabric over the cardboard, glueing the seam allowances onto the back. Place it inside the box. Stitch the inner box sides to the thimble box base as for the main box. Make sure that you don't sew too tightly into the inner box sides or they will not drop open properly when the box is finished. Glue the inner box with the thimble box attached diagonally to the base of the main box (Fig. 4).

STEP NINE

Cut the lid piece from the thick cardboard. Cut the fabric and construct the lid in the same manner as the thimble box. Cut and construct the lid lining. Glue the crazy patchwork pieced top in place. Work a row of feather stitch around the top of the lid and down each corner.

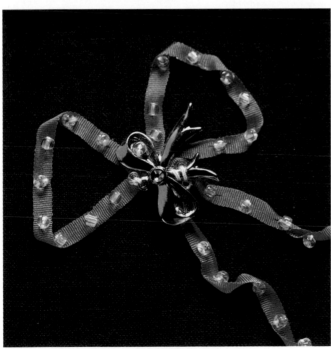

Silk ribbon held in place with seed beads

Sprig of flowers using old buttons, beads and lace

RUFFLED CUSHION

Made as a gift for a very dear friend's seventy-fifth birthday, this cushion continues the blue theme of her bedroom.

MATERIALS

40 cm (16 in) square of fabric for the base cloth

60 cm (24 in) of plain blue cotton fabric for the frill and the back

Total of 50 cm (18 in) of fancy blue and cream fabrics

20 cm (8 in) each of two different cream cotton laces

Perle cotton, Cream

Embroidery threads: Blue, Silver

Assorted cream and blue beads

Assorted buttons

Lace, braids and lace motifs

50 cm (20 in) of 7 mm ($^5/_{16}$ in) wide silver ribbon

Total of about 1 m ($1^1/_8$ yd) of silk ribbon, several shades of Blue

30 cm (12 in) zipper

Ordinary sewing thread

Crewel needle

Beading needle

Chenille needle

PREPARATION

On the wrong side of the square of base cloth fabric mark the cutting and stitching lines.

CRAZY PATCHWORK

STEP ONE

Using the Centre Patch method, crazy patch the square. Machine a row of zigzag stitches along the cutting line, then trim any excess fabric. Hand-sew a row of basting on the stitching line.

STEP TWO

Add lace or braids to cover some of the seam lines. Cover all the remaining seam lines with your choice of embroidery stitches. Embellish these rows of stitches with beads or stitch combinations of your choice. Do not bead past the row of hand-basting.

STEP THREE

Add lace motifs, ribbon embroidery, beads and buttons to complete the decoration. Stitch your name and a message, if desired.

MAKING UP

STEP ONE

Cut two pieces of the blue cotton fabric, each 20 cm x 40 cm (8 in x 16 in). Zigzag around all sides to prevent fraying. Press a 1 cm ($^3/_8$ in) hem along one of the long sides of both pieces and insert the zipper in the centre. Hand-sew the remainder of the seam. Open the zipper about half way.

STEP TWO

Cut two pieces of the blue cotton fabric, each 10 cm (4 in) by the length of the fabric. Join them into a loop. Fold the loop in half with the wrong sides together, enclosing the seams. Using the longest stitch length on your sewing machine, sew two rows of gathering 6 mm ($^1/_4$ in) apart, close to the raw edge. Determine the quarter points on the loop and mark them with pins. Pin each of these points to one of the corners of the cushion front, with the fold of the frill pointing to the middle. Carefully gather the frill to fit and stitch it in place. Zigzag or overlock the seam.

STEP THREE

On a clean surface, lay the cushion front (with the frill attached) right side up and position the cushion back (right side down) on top. Check that everything lines up, then machine-stitch all the way around, using a 1 cm ($^3/_8$ in) seam allowance. Press the seams open, clip the corners on the diagonal to reduce bulk and turn the cover right side out. Open the zipper and slip the cushion insert inside.

Tiny flowers decorate an initial

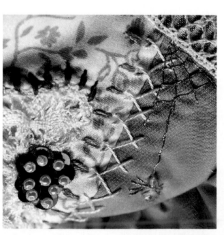

A tiny bead spider symbolises good luck

AINSLEY'S DINOSAUR

This little lady is called 'Pinkasaurus'. She is decorated only with seam embroidery so as not to detract from her unique colour and shape. You could, of course, add much more decoration if you wish.

MATERIALS

White paper
Pencil
Ruler
60 cm (²/₃ yd) of poplin or sheeting for the base cloth
Total of approximately 50 cm (20 in) of coordinating pink fabrics
25 cm (10 in) of pale pink satin
1 m (1¹/₈ yd) of narrow white braid
Lace
30 cm (12 in) of 1.2 cm (¹/₂ in) wide satin ribbon, Pale Pink
Matching sewing thread
Stranded cotton or Perle cotton, main colour
Assorted embroidery threads to tone or contrast
Metallic thread, Pink
Silk ribbons
Assorted beads
Crewel needle
Chenille needle
Beading needle
200–300 g of polyester fibre fill
Set of bear joints, 40 mm (1¹/₂ in) in diameter, or four buttons
Dental floss
Two 1 cm (³/₈ in) self-cover buttons
80 cm (32 in) of 4 cm (1¹/₂ in) wide satin ribbon, Pink
Thick cardboard or plastic (an ice-cream container is ideal)
Craft glue

CRAZY PATCHWORK

See the pattern on the Pull Out Pattern Sheet.

STEP ONE

Trace, then cut out the pattern pieces. Using the Set Pattern method, transfer all the pattern shapes and details, then cut out and crazy patch all the pieces.

STEP TWO

Once the base cloth is pieced, turn it over and machine a line of stitching on the outer line previously drawn. Hand-baste a row of stitches on the inner line.

STEP THREE

Add lace and/or braid to cover some of the seams. Cover all the remaining seams with your choice of embroidery stitches. Embellish these rows of stitches with added beads or stitch combinations. Do not bead outside the basting line.

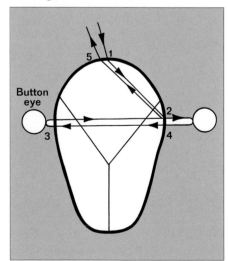

MAKING UP

STEP ONE

Pin and stitch the four sets of inner and outer legs, each from toe to heel. Following the instructions for the type of joints you are using, insert the appropriate part of each joint into each leg at the position marked on the inner leg. Set the legs aside.

STEP TWO

Place two tail sections together with the right sides facing and stitch. Press the seams and turn the tail right side out.

STEP THREE

Matching the notches, pin then stitch the head gusset to one side of the head. Repeat for the other side.

STEP FOUR

Matching the notches, pin then stitch the body gusset to one side of the body. Repeat for the other side.

STEP FIVE

Carefully stitch the nose-to-chest seam. Stitch the back seam from the head gusset to the large dot.

STEP SIX

Place the tail in position and stitch it to one side only, leaving an opening for inserting the filling.

STEP SEVEN

Turn up the seam allowance on the bottom of the leg and baste to hold it in place. Using small pieces at a time, insert the filling into the legs, paying particular attention to the area around the joints. Continue to add filling until the leg won't hold any more. For a stiffer foot pad, cut a piece of cardboard or plastic slightly smaller than the paper foot pad pattern. Glue a little filling onto one side of the cardboard or plastic, then carefully position the foot pad on top. Glue the seam allowance of the foot pad around the underside of the cardboard or plastic. Matching the heel and toe seams and the two appropriate points on the foot pad, sew several stitches to hold the foot pad in place. Use basting stitches to ease the leg and the foot pad to a good fit. Stitch half the foot pad to the leg, using very small stitches and being sure to catch both layers of material. Continue to add filling until the foot is very firm, then complete the seam

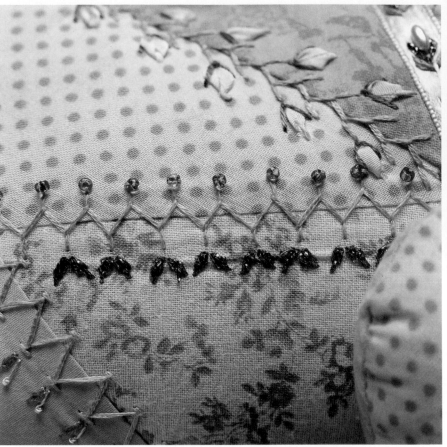

Decoration is limited to seam embroidery and beading

STEP EIGHT

Begin filling the head, using small pieces of filling at a time. If you put too big a piece in, it tends to go lumpy. Poke the filling firmly into the nose/mouth area with a chopstick or spoon handle. Add the filling until the head, neck and part of the chest are firm.

STEP NINE

Attach the legs to the positions marked (see page 30 of Teddy Bear instructions).

STEP TEN

Add more filling until the body is firm and the filling is trying to escape through the opening. Thread a needle with sewing thread and sew several back stitches in the seam allowance at the bottom of the side with the tail attached. Bring the needle and thread to the outside. Sew about one-quarter of the opening closed, using ladder stitch. Be careful to stitch through both sides and the tail. Add some more filling, then sew another quarter of the

opening closed. Repeat this step until the opening is completely closed, taking care to add enough filling so the dinosaur doesn't have a saggy or rumpled-looking bottom.

STEP ELEVEN

Cover the buttons in a scrap of dark pink fabric, following the manufacturer's instructions. Thread a 50 cm (20 in) length of dental floss and double it in the needle. Insert the needle into the head at the head/gusset seam leaving about 4 cm (1½ in) exposed. Bring the needle out at the position of one of the eyes. Stitch three back stitches, one on top of the other, then pick up one button, pass the needle through the head to the other eye position and pick up the other button. Return to where the thread came out at the first eye (Fig. 1). Pull up the thread tightly so the eyes are embedded into the head a little. Wind the thread around the shank of the first eye and tie it off with a smocking knot (or any other knot you know to be very safe). Pass

the needle back through the head and out close to where you put it in. Pull up both threads and cut them off close to the surface. The ends should pop back inside the head.

STEP TWELVE

Thread a 60 cm (24 in) length of metallic thread and make a double knot approximately 3 cm (1¼ in) from the end. Insert the needle at the mouth and pass it up to where the nose will be. Using satin stitch, sew the nose before returning the needle as close to the mouth entry point as possible. Sew a smocking knot or tie a very secure one as close to the fabric as possible. Cut the thread, leaving a tail for the tongue.

STEP THIRTEEN

Using the wide satin ribbon, tie a bow around the neck and give your dinosaur a name.

CHRISTMAS DECORATIONS

These charming little decorations have been made in traditional red, green and gold, but you can make them in any colour combination that takes your fancy. Quick to make, they would make a lovely gift.

MATERIALS

For the stocking
White paper
60 cm (20 in) of red cotton fabric
30 cm x 60 cm (12 in x 24 in) of
    fabric for the base cloth
40 cm (16 in) of 12 mm (¹/₂ in) wide
    satin ribbon, Red
1.8 m (2 yd) of red piping
Assorted fancy fabrics, such as
    Christmas prints and satins
Ordinary sewing thread
Embroidery threads to match or
    contrast with the fabrics
Embroidery thread, Gold
Lace, braid, ribbons
Silk ribbons in colours and widths for
    embroidery
Assorted beads, buttons and charms
For a set of six decorations
25 cm (10 in) of fabric for the base
    cloth
Total of 30 cm (12 in) of fancy fabrics
Rayon embroidery thread: Red,
    Green, Cream
Embroidery thread, Gold
Gold beads
Sequins: red, green and gold
Gold rickrack braid
40 cm (16 in) each of thin cord: red,
    green and gold
Polyester fibre fill
Ordinary sewing thread, White
Crewel needle
Beading needle

CHRISTMAS STOCKING

PREPARATION

See the pattern on the Pull Out Pattern Sheet.

Trace the pattern. Using the pattern, cut one stocking from the base cloth fabric, allowing an extra 3 cm (1 in) all round. On the wrong side, mark the stitching and cutting lines. Cut three stockings from the red fabric and set them aside.

CRAZY PATCHWORK

STEP ONE

Using the Random Block method, crazy patch the stocking front. Machine a row of zigzag stitches along the cutting line, then trim the excess fabric. Hand-sew a row of basting on the stitching line.

STEP TWO

Add lace or braid to cover some of the seam lines. Cover all the remaining seam lines with embroidery stitches.

These Christmas decorations will become family heirlooms

A detail of the middle of the stocking

Embellish these rows of stitches with beads or stitch combinations. Do not bead past the row of hand-basting.

STEP THREE

Add lace motifs, ribbon embroidery, beads and buttons to complete the decoration. Stitch your name and a message, if desired.

MAKING UP

STEP ONE

Place the stocking front right side up on a table. Pin the piping down the sides and around the bottom. Start at the top of the right-hand side and aim to place the row of stitching that holds the piping cord inside the material exactly on the row of stitches hand-basted earlier. Using the zipper foot on the sewing machine, carefully stitch the piping to the stocking front, clipping the piping (but not the stocking) as you go around the curves. Aim to stitch on top of, or as close as possible to, the row of stitching on the piping.

STEP TWO

Place the stocking front right side up on a table with the stocking back on top. Align the edges and pin them carefully together. Stitch them together, stitching exactly on the piping stitching line. Trim the edges. Clip the curves and press carefully. Turn the stocking right side out.

STEP THREE

Pin the piping to the top of the stocking in the same way as before, then stitch.

STEP FOUR

For the lining, place the two remaining pieces with the right sides together. Stitch the sides and the bottom, leaving an opening in one side as indicated on the pattern. Clip the curves and press the seams open carefully. Do not turn. Carefully place the stocking into the lining, matching side seams. Fold the satin ribbon in half and sandwich it between the stocking and the lining on the back seam.

STEP FIVE

Using the zipper foot and following the same procedure as before, sew the stocking and the lining together at the top. Press the seams open carefully and turn the stocking to the right side pulling it out through the opening in the lining seam. Slipstitch the opening closed. Push the lining back down inside the stocking, taking particular

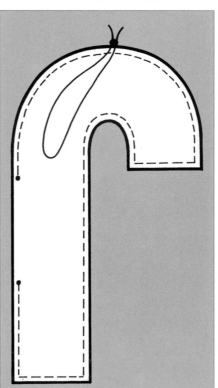

Fig. 1

care to align the toes and heels of the main piece and the lining. Carefully press the top seam from the outside.

SMALL DECORATIONS

CRAZY PATCHWORK

See the patterns on the Pull Out Pattern Sheet.

STEP ONE

Trace the patterns and, using the method marked on each pattern, crazy patch all the shapes.
Note: For each decoration, you will need one shape and its mirror-reverse.

STEP TWO

Add rickrack braid to some of the seams. Cover all the remaining seams with embroidery stitches in colours matched to the fabric. Decorate these seams with beads, sequins and stitch combinations as desired.

MAKING UP

STEP ONE

Cut 20 cm (8 in) lengths of appropriately coloured cord, then knot the ends together. Place the cord on one side of the shape at the X, with the loop lying over the body of the shape and the knot positioned so it will be in the seam allowance (Fig. 1). Using a small stitch, machine-sew the shapes together with the right sides facing, leaving an opening for filling as marked on the pattern. Clip the curves and clip into the corners. Trim the bulk at the points. Turn the pieces right side out.

STEP TWO

Carefully add the filling, poking it right into the corners. Sew the opening closed with small ladder stitches.

WAISTCOAT

Head-turning waistcoats can be personalised with buttons, beads and embroidered initials.

MATERIALS

Commercial pattern (without darts)
50 cm (20 in) of fabric for the base cloth
Total of 50 cm (20 in) of fancy fabrics for the fronts
Fabric for the lining
Tissue or tracing paper
Stranded cotton, Very Pale Mauve
Assorted embroidery threads to match or contrast with the fabrics
Metallic embroidery thread, Silver
Assorted silk ribbons to match or contrast with the fabrics
Assorted beads, between three and five different kinds
Sequins, buttons and charms
Lace motifs
Three 1 cm (³/₈ in) press studs
Ordinary sewing thread to match the lining, and White
Crewel needles
Beading needles
Chenille needles

PREPARATION

STEP ONE

Trace the required pieces from the commercial pattern onto the tissue or tracing paper and cut them out.

STEP TWO

Pin the front pattern to the base cloth fabric. Transfer the cutting line and the stitching lines to the wrong sides of the fabric. Cut out, leaving an additional 2 cm (³/₄ in) all round. Transfer all the lines to both pattern pieces.

CRAZY PATCHWORK

STEP ONE

Work with the right side of the base cloth fabric facing up and the lines drawn on the underside. Using the Random Block method, crazy patch both front pieces.

On the wrong side of the patchwork, stitch a row of machine-stitching on the cutting line and hand-sew a line of basting on the stitching line.

EMBELLISHING

STEP ONE

Cover all the seams with your choice of embroidery stitches. Embellish these rows of stitches with beads and/or stitch combinations. Do not bead outside the basting lines.

STEP TWO

Fill the plain fabric patches with additional embroidery stitches in either silk or cotton thread, or a combination of both. Add beads, buttons, charms, lace motifs and so on.

STEP THREE

Sign and date your work somewhere unobtrusive.

White silk ribbon roses and buds

Purple sequins and beads decorate an initial

MAKING UP

STEP ONE

With the sewing machine set to a fine zigzag stitch, sew over the row of machine stitches and carefully cut away the excess fabric.

STEP TWO

Complete the vest, following the pattern instructions. Topstitch 6 mm ($^1/_4$ in) from the edge, taking extreme care near beads, buttons or sequins.

STEP THREE

Stitch on the press studs. On the front, disguise them with groups of beads.

Pink silk flowers and sequins atop a seahorse charm

A silver dolphin button among purple ribbon flowers

Snowdrops stitched in silk ribbon

Silver ribbon, gathered along one edge, forms flowers

56

FRINGED EVENING BAG

This beautiful little evening bag, beaded and glamorous, is just
right for the theatre or a special party.

MATERIALS

Tracing paper
Pencil
30 cm (12 in) square of black velvet
30 cm (12 in) square of black poplin
30 cm (12 in) square of lightweight
    fabric for the base cloth
Scraps of seven assorted black
    fabrics
Ordinary sewing thread, Black
DMC rayon embroidery thread,
    Silver
Assorted embroidery threads: Silver,
    White
Assorted beads: silver, black
Sequins, black
Buttons and charms
Lace motifs
30 cm (12 in) of 7 mm ($^5/_{16}$ in) wide
    silk ribbon, White
50 cm (18 in) of 3 mm ($^3/_{16}$ in) silk
    ribbon, White
Silver bag frame
Dental floss
Black permanent marker pen
Beading needle
Chenille needle
Crewel needle

For the fringe
One packet of 3 mm ($^3/_{16}$ in) black
    beads
One packet of 2 mm ($^1/_{16}$ in) silver
    pearls
One packet of 2 mm ($^1/_{16}$ in) silver-
    lined seed beads
One packet of 5 mm ($^1/_4$ in) black-
    faceted beads
One packet of 3 mm ($^3/_{16}$ in) silver
    bugle beads
One packet of 5 mm ($^1/_4$ in) flat black
    disc beads

PREPARATION

See the pattern on the Pull Out Pattern
Sheet.

Trace the pattern, then cut out one
back from the black velvet and two lining pieces from the black poplin. Cut
one piece from the base cloth fabric,
allowing an extra 2 cm ($^3/_4$ in) all round.
Transfer the pattern markings to the
base cloth.

CRAZY PATCHWORK

STEP ONE

Using the Centre Patch method, piece
the base cloth using the fancy black
fabrics. Stitch a row of machine-
stitches on the cutting line and hand-
sew a row of basting stitches on the
sewing line. Cover all the seams with
your choice of embroidery stitches,
using the rayon thread. Embellish
these rows of stitches with beads or
stitch combinations of your choice. Do
not bead outside the hand-basting.

Silk ribbon roses shine on a black background

Add lace motifs, ribbon embroidery, tassels, beads and buttons. Note that the two end buttons near the hinge are added only after the bag is made up and sewn to the frame.

❤ MAKING UP

STEP ONE

Place the bag front and the velvet back together with the right sides facing and sew around the edges between the two large dots. Reinforce the stitching over the dots with a second row of stitches on top of the first row. Clip the curves carefully, then press the seams open. Turn the bag right side out. Repeat with the poplin linings. Clip the curves but leave the lining inside out.

STEP TWO

Carefully hold the bag against the frame and adjust for an exact fit, if necessary, then finger press the seam allowances to the inside and baste them in place. Repeat with the lining.

STEP THREE

Baste the exact centre front and back of the bag to the exact centre front and back of the frame. Check again that the sides of the bag exactly match the sides of the frame.

STEP FOUR

Fit the lining inside the bag and align the centre front and centre back, and the sides. Pin or baste the lining to the bag, 1 cm ($^3/_8$ in) below the top edge. Using the dental floss and starting at the hinge, stitch the lining and the bag to the frame through the holes in the frame. Stitch a sequin and a bead at each hole (Fig. 1). Paint out any visible dental floss with the marker pen.

STEP FIVE

Thread the beading needle with approximately 140 cm (55 in) of thread. Knot the ends together. Determine the exact centre of the bottom of the bag and begin at this point, as close to the seam line as possible, and work from the centre to one side, then from the centre to the other side. Sew two tiny stitches, one on top of the other, then, following the bead order indicated in figure 2, thread the beads onto the thread. Push the beads along until they reach the bag, but leave a tiny space so the fringe will swing. Take the needle back up through the beads, using the last bead as a stopper. Make sure the beads are sitting neatly in line, then secure them with two small stitches and a knot. Stitch a 'spacer' bead in place, then make another strand of the fringe. Continue in this way, taking care to secure each one with stitches and a knot.

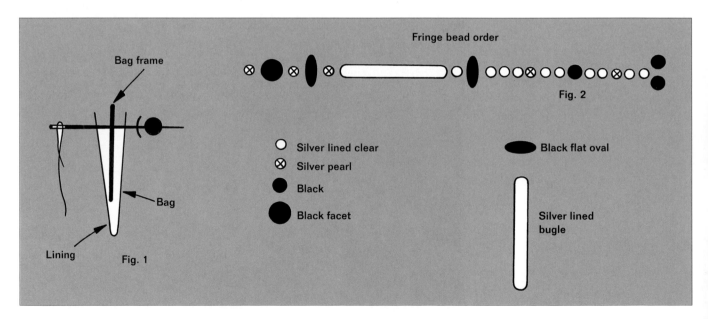

Fringe bead order

Bag frame

Bag

Lining   Fig. 1

Fig. 2

○ Silver lined clear
⊗ Silver pearl
● Black
⬤ Black facet

⬬ Black flat oval

▯ Silver lined bugle

JEWELLERY POUCH

Pockets on the inside, crazy patchwork on the outside, this beautiful jewellery pouch will be a lovely addition to your dressing table.

MATERIALS

60 cm (24 in) square of fabric for the base cloth

1 m (1¹/₈ yd) of dusty pink satin for the lining and frill

1 m (1¹/₈ yd) of dusty pink homespun

50 cm (20 in) of Pellon or thin wadding

3 m (3³/₈ yd) of pink cord

Total of 70 cm (28 in) square of assorted fancy fabrics

Embroidery threads to contrast with or match the fabrics

Lace, braid and lace motifs

Assorted beads, buttons and charms

Variety of silk ribbons

15 cm (6 in) square of thick cardboard or template plastic (an ice-cream container is ideal)

20 cm (8 in) square of wadding

Craft glue

Ordinary sewing thread

Crewel needle

Beading needle

Chenille needle

PREPARATION

STEP ONE

Cut a circle with a diameter of 58 cm (22³/₄ in) from the base cloth fabric. On the wrong side, mark the cutting and stitching lines. Draw in the cutting line 2 cm (³/₄ in) from the edge and the sewing line 1 cm (³/₈ in) inside that.

STEP TWO

For the pocket, cut a circle with a diameter of 35 cm (14 in) from the homespun and another one the same size from the satin. For the lining, cut a circle with a diameter of 58 cm (22³/₄ in). From the Pellon, cut a circle 49 cm (19 in) in diameter. From the thick cardboard or template plastic, cut a circle 12 cm (4³/₄ in) in diameter.

CRAZY PATCHWORK

STEP ONE

On the right side of the base cloth and using a combination of the Centre Patch method and the Random Block method, cover the base cloth with crazy patchwork using the fancy fabrics. You may like to include some of the lining as one of the fancy fabrics.

STEP TWO

Once the base cloth is pieced, turn it over and machine a line of stitching on the cutting line and hand-baste a row of stitches on the stitching line.

STEP THREE

Add lace and/or braid to cover some of the seams. Cover all the remaining seams with your choice of embroidery stitches. Embellish these rows of stitches with beads or stitch combinations. Do not bead outside the basting line.

STEP FOUR

Fill the patches of plain fabric with embroidery, beads, buttons, charms

Silk ribbon fuchsias in a variety of colours

and lace motifs. Sign and date your work, if desired.

STEP FIVE

Using a fine machine zigzag stitch, sew over the row of machine-stitching made earlier. Trim away all excess material carefully. Set the pieces aside.

MAKING UP

STEP ONE

For the pocket, stitch together the homespun and the satin circles with the right sides facing, leaving a 5 cm (2 in) opening. Clip the curves, then press and turn the piece right side out. Slipstitch the opening closed. Fold the circle into quarters and finger press to mark the centre.

STEP TWO

Fold the homespun circle into quarters and finger press to mark the centre.

STEP THREE

Glue a layer of wadding onto one side of the cardboard or plastic circle, then trim away any excess.

STEP FOUR

Place the Pellon circle, already cut, on the table and stack the other pieces in the following order: large homespun circle, cardboard or plastic circle with the wadding side up, satin/homespun circle with the satin side up. Centre all the layers carefully, then stitch all the layers together, using the zipper foot on the sewing machine, with the row of stitching as close to the edge of the cardboard/plastic circle as possible. Take care not to stitch through the cardboard/plastic.

STEP FIVE

Lay the joined circles flat on the table with the Pellon side down and mark eight, ten or twelve equal pockets on the satin/homespun circle. Stitch from the edge of the cardboard/plastic circle to the edge of the satin/home-

spun circle. Pull all the thread ends to the back and secure them carefully.

STEP SIX

From the satin, cut a bias strip 6 cm (2³⁄₈ in) wide and 170 cm (67 in) long. Join several bias strips, if necessary, to achieve the required length. Cut the strip in half, then rejoin it, leaving a 1 cm (³⁄₈ in) opening in the centre of this seam.

STEP SEVEN

Fold the completed crazy patchwork in half and mark the folds with pins. These two pins will be a guide for the openings for the cord. Pin the bias strip carefully around the edge of the crazy patchwork, placing the seam with the opening exactly over one of the pins. Work around in one direction then the other until you reach the second pin. Carefully stitch the ends of the bias strip together, allowing for the bias, and again leaving a 1 cm (³⁄₈ in) opening in the centre of this seam. Stitch the bias strip in place, clip the curves and press carefully. Topstitch 2 mm (¹⁄₁₆ in) on the satin side of the seam.

STEP EIGHT

From the satin, cut a bias strip 6 cm (2¹⁄₂ in) wide and 190 cm (75 in) long. Join bias strips as necessary to achieve the required length. Fold the strip in half lengthwise and press.

STEP NINE

Place the pocket unit face down on the table and centre the crazy patchwork on top, smoothing out any wrinkles. Pin the pieces together and trim away any excess fabric to make the two pieces even. Using the zipper foot and a seam allowance of 6 mm (¹⁄₄ in), stitch the doubled raw edges of the bias binding to both pieces. Turn and slipstitch the fold of the bias binding to the seam line as invisibly as possible.

STEP TEN

To make the cord channel, stitch 2.5 cm (1 in) from the outer edge, through both layers. Cut the cord in half, then insert the cords from opposite openings so each cord goes in one opening, around through the channel and out the same opening. Knot the cord ends together. Add a few decorative beads to the cords, if desired.

Bullion stitch bunnies in a field of forget-me-nots

WALLHANGING

By joining crazy patchwork blocks together in the same manner as traditional blocks, Theresia has made her grandson Shannon a wallhanging any Elvis fan would love.

MATERIALS

1 m (1$\frac{1}{8}$ yd) of fabric for the base cloth

1.5 m (1$\frac{2}{3}$ yd) of black cotton fabric for the backing and the edge strips

3.4 m (3$\frac{3}{4}$ yd) of 4 cm (1$\frac{1}{2}$ in) wide black grosgrain ribbon

4 m (4$\frac{1}{2}$ yd) of black satin bias binding

Total of 1 m (1$\frac{1}{8}$ yd) of assorted fancy fabrics

Embroidery threads

Ordinary sewing thread

Laces and braids

Assorted beads, buttons, charms etc

Crewel needle

Beading needle

PREPARATION

Using the dimensions given in figure 1, cut the required pieces from the base cloth fabric, allowing an additional 2 cm ($\frac{3}{4}$ in) all round each piece.

CRAZY PATCHWORK

STEP ONE

Using the Centre Patch method or any combination of methods, crazy patch the nine blocks for the wallhanging. On each block, machine a row of zigzag stitches along the cutting line, then trim any excess fabric. Hand-sew a row of basting on the stitching line.

STEP TWO

Add lace or braids to cover some seam lines. Cover the remaining seam lines with your choice of embroidery stitches. Embellish these rows of stitches with beads or stitch combinations. Do not bead past the row of hand-basting. Add lace motifs, ribbon embroidery, beads and buttons to complete the decoration. Stitch on your name and a message, if desired.

MAKING UP

STEP ONE

Cut the following pieces from the backing fabric: one piece 95 cm (37$\frac{1}{2}$ in) square, two pieces 8 cm x 95 cm (3$\frac{1}{4}$ in x 37$\frac{1}{2}$ in) and two pieces 8 cm x 84 cm (3$\frac{1}{4}$ in x 33 in).

STEP TWO

Lay the backing cloth right side down on a table (or the floor if you don't have a table big enough). Pin the crazy patchwork blocks in position.

STEP THREE

Cut grosgrain ribbon to the following lengths: two pieces 84 cm (33 in), four pieces 33 cm (13 in) and two pieces 16 cm (6$\frac{1}{4}$ in). Pin all the horizontal ribbons in place, then stitch them down through all the layers.

Forget-me-nots in silk ribbon French knots

STEP FOUR

Pin, then stitch in place the two vertical ribbons. Pin, then stitch the top and bottom edge strips in place. Pin, then stitch the two side edge strips in place.

STEP FIVE

Place the satin bias binding on the quilt front with the right sides together and stitch through all the layers. Slipstitch the other edge of the bias binding to the backing, as close as possible to the first row of stitches.

STEP SIX

Turn under a hem at the ends of the remaining length of grosgrain ribbon and stitch it in place to form a pocket for the hanging rod.

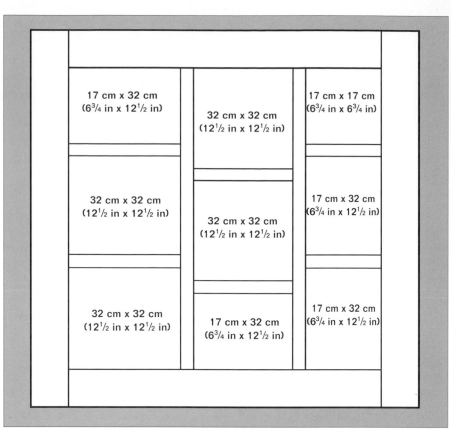

17 cm x 32 cm
(6¾ in x 12½ in)

32 cm x 32 cm
(12½ in x 12½ in)

17 cm x 17 cm
(6¾ in x 6¾ in)

32 cm x 32 cm
(12½ in x 12½ in)

32 cm x 32 cm
(12½ in x 12½ in)

17 cm x 32 cm
(6¾ in x 12½ in)

32 cm x 32 cm
(12½ in x 12½ in)

17 cm x 32 cm
(6¾ in x 12½ in)

17 cm x 32 cm
(6¾ in x 12½ in)

Measurements are completed base cloth sizes

Purple wisteria using French knots worked close together

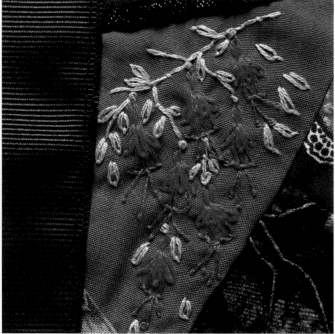

Fuchsias worked in pink stranded cotton

64

Gramophone from Flash Trash, Camperdown

FISH CUSHION

Appliqué a crazy patchwork fish onto a silk cushion.

MATERIALS

White paper
Pencil
Tracing paper
30 cm (12 in) square of gold satin
Total of 20 cm (8 in) square of ten
    different blue fabrics
35 cm (14 in) of cream dupion silk
35 cm (14 in) of white poplin or lawn
30 cm (12 in) zipper
30 cm (12 in) cushion insert
1.2 m (1$\frac{1}{3}$ yd) of old gold fringed
    braid
30 cm (12 in) square of lightweight
    iron-on interfacing
30 cm (12 in) square of fabric for the
    base cloth
Embroidery thread: Gold, Cream
Rayon or other fancy embroidery
    thread, Blue
Blue seed beads and bugle beads
Assorted beads
Crewel needle
Beading needle
Ordinary sewing thread, White

PREPARATION

See the pattern on the Pull Out Pattern
Sheet.

Trace the pattern onto white paper and
again onto tracing paper. From the
tracing paper pattern, cut out the sections to be crazy patched. Using these
as templates, cut two base cloth pieces
with a 1 cm (3/8 in) seam allowance.

CRAZY PATCHWORK

Using postage-stamp-sized pieces of
the blue fabrics, crazy patch the two
sections, using the Narrow Strip
method. Cover all the seams with your
choice of embroidery stitches. Embellish these rows of stitches with beads
or stitch combinations. Keep your
stitches small or they will overwhelm
the small pieces of fabric.

MAKING UP

STEP ONE

Using the tracing paper templates as a
guide, turn, then baste the outer seam
allowance under.

STEP TWO

Cut the iron-on interfacing to fit the
paper tracing exactly. Make sure the
interfacing is iron-on side up, or the
whole thing will be reversed and the
appliqué pieces won't fit. Iron the interfacing onto the wrong side of the gold
satin and cut it out, leaving a 6 mm
(1/4 in) seam allowance. Baste the seam
allowance under, close to the edge.

STEP THREE

Referring to the pattern, position the
crazy patchwork pieces. Pin them in
place and adjust the shape, if necessary. Blind stitch the pieces in place,
using tiny stitches through all layers.

STEP FOUR

Form the eye by buttonhole stitching
around a metal button, then stitch the
button into position.

STEP FIVE

Cut a piece of dupion silk 32 cm
(12$\frac{1}{2}$ in) square. Machine-zigzag all
the edges to prevent fraying. Fold the
square into quarters to determine the
exact centre. Fold the paper fish template into quarters and put in a pin at
the centre point. Pin the fish carefully
into place on the silk, matching the
centres and putting the pins as close to
the edges as possible. Blind stitch it in
place. Stitch a row of feather stitch right
around the fish to hide any pin marks
and the appliqué stitches. Use bugle
and seed beads to define the fins.

STEP SIX

Cut two pieces of dupion silk, each
18 cm x 32 cm (7 in x 12$\frac{1}{2}$ in). Machine-
zigzag around all the sides to prevent
fraying. Press a 1 cm (3/8 in) hem along
one of the long sides of both pieces,
and insert the zipper in the centre.
Hand-sew the seam ends. Open the
zipper about half way.

STEP SEVEN

Place the poplin or lawn on a clean
surface with the cushion front (right
side up) over it, then the cushion back
(right side down) on top of that. Check
that everything lines up, then machine-
stitch all the way around using a 1 cm
(3/8 in) seam allowance. Press the
seams open, clip the corners on the
diagonal to reduce bulk, then turn the
cushion right side out.

STEP EIGHT

Fold under 6 mm (1/4 in) of braid and,
starting at the bottom centre next to the
zipper, hand-stitch the braid around
the cushion as invisibly as possible. At
the finishing end, fold under 6 mm
(1/4 in) and, using tiny stitches, join the
two ends together. Open the zipper
fully, slip the cushion insert inside, then
close the zipper.

PADDED COATHANGER

A special gift for a special lady, made in her favourite colours.

MATERIALS

Adult-sized wooden coathanger
White paper
15 cm x 50 cm (6 in x 20 in) of fabric
   for the base cloth
15 cm x 50 cm (6 in x 20 in) of fancy
   fabric for the back
1.2 m (1⅓ yd) of matching satin
   piping
1.5 m (1⅔ yd) of 10 cm (4 in) wide
   soft wadding
25 cm x 50 cm (10 in x 20 in) of
   wadding
Total of 15 cm x 50 cm (6 in x 20 in)
   of assorted fancy fabrics
Ordinary sewing thread
Laces, lace motifs, silk ribbons and
   braids
Rayon embroidery thread to match
   and contrast with the fabrics
Assorted beads, buttons, charms
Crewel needle
Beading needle
Chenille needle

PREPARATION

See the pattern on the Pull Out Pattern
Sheet.

STEP ONE

Trace the pattern onto the white paper.
Transfer all the markings.

STEP TWO

Cut one coathanger from the base
cloth fabric 3 cm (1 in) larger all round
than the pattern. On the wrong side,
mark the stitching and cutting lines.
Cut one coathanger from fancy fabric
and set it aside.

CRAZY PATCHWORK

STEP ONE

Using the Random Block method or the
Narrow Strip method, crazy patch the
coathanger front. Machine a row of
zigzag stitches along the cutting line,
trim any excess fabric. Hand-sew a
row of basting stitches on the marked
stitching line.

STEP TWO

Add lace or braids to cover some of
the seam lines. Cover all the remaining
seam lines with your choice of embroidery stitches. Embellish these rows of
stitches with beads or stitch combinations of your choice. Do not bead past
the row of hand-basting.

Blue button flowers

Purple heather in flat rayon ribbon

68

Add lace motifs, ribbon embroidery, beads and buttons to complete the decoration. Stitch your name and a message, if desired.

MAKING UP

STEP ONE

Cut the 25 cm x 50 cm (10 in x 20 in) piece of wadding in half lengthwise so that each piece is 12.5 cm x 50 cm (5 in x 20 in). Place the coathanger front face up on top of one piece. Pin them together. Beginning at **A** and leaving 1 cm (³/₈ in) free, pin the piping over the row of hand-basting. Aim to have the stitching line on the piping exactly on top of (or as close as possible to) the hand-basting. Using the zipper foot on the sewing machine, stitch around to **B**. Cut off the excess piping, leaving a 1 cm (³/₈ in) tail, and clipping the piping seam allowance (but not the fabric) at the curves for a smooth, rounded edge. Turn the ends of the piping out away from the fabric. Back stitch for security at points **A** and **B** (Fig. 1).

STEP TWO

Lay the front on the table with the patchwork side up. Lay the back on top with the right sides together, and place the second piece of wadding on top. Pin the pieces to hold them together. Turn the whole thing over so the piping stitching row is visible and, sewing exactly on top of the piping stitching, join the front to the back from **A** to **a** and from **b** to **B**. Back stitch for security at **A** and **B**. Trim the excess wadding and fabric from the seam line and carefully press the seam open. Trim any fabric and wadding that will be outside the lower seam allowance when it is stitched. Turn the hanger cover right side out.

STEP THREE

Insert the hook part way into the hole in the wooden hanger, then wind the long narrow strip of wadding around the hanger. Begin next to the hook and wind to one end then right back to the other end before returning to the centre. Overlap the wadding as you wind to give a plump hanger. Trim any excess wadding and secure it with a few stitches, particularly at the ends.

STEP FOUR

Remove the cord from inside the remaining piping and cut off a 10 cm (4 in) length. Stitch one end closed. Remove the hook from the hanger and carefully slip it into the piping tube.

STEP FIVE

Place the padded hanger into the cover. Reinsert the hook and pull the piping tube firm before securing it with a few stitches. Turn under the seam allowances and slipstitch the opening closed on the back of the hanger.

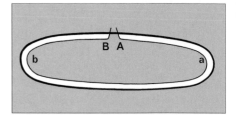

Fig. 1

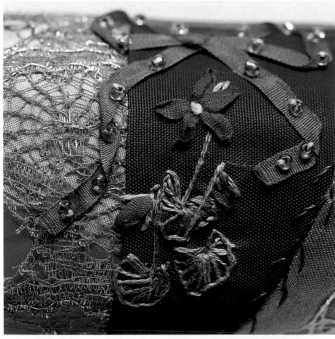

Silk ribbon violets nestle under a ribbon and bead bow

A 'good luck' spider in its web

ARMCHAIR CADDY

This lovely sewing companion slips easily over the arm of your
favourite chair and will keep all your threads tidy.

MATERIALS

Tracing paper
50 cm (20 in) of pink cotton
   (headcloth or patchwork weight)
2 m (2¼ yd) of pink bias binding
20 cm x 70 cm (8 in x 28 in) of fabric
   for the base cloth
Total of 30 cm x 60 cm (12 in x 24 in)
   of assorted fancy fabrics
Ordinary sewing thread
Polyester fibre fill
Lace, lace motifs, braids and silk
   ribbons
Rayon embroidery thread, Pink
Assorted embroidery threads to
   match and contrast with the fabrics
Assorted beads, buttons and charms
1 m (1⅛ yd) of 7 mm (⁵/₁₆ in) wide
   satin ribbon, Dusty Pink
Crewel needle
Beading needle

PREPARATION

See the pattern on the Pull Out Pattern
Sheet.

STEP ONE

Trace the pattern, transferring all the
lines and markings. Trace two pocket
fronts and one pincushion onto the
base cloth fabric. Transfer the markings for the stitching lines and the cutting lines to the wrong side. Cut out,
leaving an additional 2 cm (³/₄ in)
allowance all round. Cut out a rectangle
18 cm x 20 cm (7 in x 8 in) for the
pincushion.

STEP TWO

Cut two caddies and two pocket linings
from the pink fabric. On each caddy,
transfer the markings for the stitching
line and hand-baste a row of stitches
along this line.

CRAZY PATCHWORK

STEP ONE

Using the Centre Patch method, crazy
patch the fronts and the pincushion. On
the wrong side, machine a row of
zigzag stitches along the cutting line.
Trim any excess fabric. Hand-sew a
row of basting on the stitching line.

Old buttons, beads and folded ribbon roses feature on this piece

71

STEP TWO

Add lace or braids to cover some of the seam lines. Cover all the remaining seam lines with your choice of embroidery stitches. Embellish these rows of stitches with beads or stitch combinations. Add lace motifs, ribbon embroidery, beads and buttons.

MAKING UP

STEP ONE

Fold the pincushion in half lengthwise with the right sides together, then stitch the ends to make a tube. Turn the tube right side out and roll it until the seam is at the centre back, then stitch one end closed. Fill the pincushion, making it fairly firm, but not hard. Stitch the other end closed.

STEP TWO

Place the pocket and pocket linings wrong sides together. Pin to hold. Pin, then stitch one side of the bias binding to the right side of the crazy pocket edge. Turn the pocket over and slipstitch the other edge of the bias

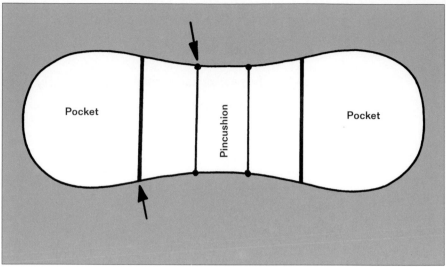

Fig. 1

binding to the pocket lining. Place these stitches on top of, or as close as possible to, the machine-stitching line. Repeat for the other pocket.

STEP THREE

Place the two caddy pieces on the table, then pin the pocket/lining pieces in position on top. Pin, then baste the pincushion between the dots, in the centre of the caddy. Open out the bias binding. Pin it on the assembled caddy so the seam allowance fold line sits

exactly on top of the row of hand-basting. Using the zipper foot on the sewing machine, stitch the bias binding to the caddy through all the layers, catching the ends of the pincushion. Slipstitch the other side of the bias binding to the back of the caddy. Aim to have these stitches on top of, or as close as possible to, the row of machine-stitching.

72

WELL-DRESSED TOYS

Dressed to impress, Teddy, Rabbit and Dolly show off their clothes.

Note: The dress and apron are made to fit a 50 cm (20 in) doll and the vest fits a 30 cm (12 in) bear. You can make the vest smaller or larger by reducing or enlarging the pattern.

MATERIALS

For the dress

30 cm (12 in) of prewashed calico
Total of 30 cm (12 in) square of
    assorted fancy fabrics
Three 6 mm ($^1/_4$ in) buttons
Two 3 mm ($^1/_8$ in) buttons
15 cm (6 in) of narrow bias binding

For the apron

30 cm x 45 cm (12 in x18 in) of fabric
    for the base cloth
1.85 m (2 yd) of white bias binding
Total of 30 cm x 45 cm (12 in x 18 in)
    of scraps of six or eight fancy
    fabrics
Laces, lace motifs and braids
Beads and buttons
Two 6 mm ($^1/_4$ in) white buttons

For the vest

15 cm x 30 cm (6 in x 12 in) of fabric
    for the base cloth
30 cm x 60 cm (12 in x 24 in) of plain
    fabric for the back and the lining
Total of 15 cm x 30 cm (6 in x 12 in)
    of scraps of six or eight fancy
    fabrics
Laces, braids and silk ribbons
Assorted beads and buttons
Embroidery thread to match or
    contrast with the fabrics
Crewel needle
Straw needle or milliner's needle

For all three

Tracing paper
Pencil
Rayon embroidery thread, White
Six small silver press studs
Ordinary sewing thread

PREPARATION

See the patterns on the Pull Out Pattern Sheet.

DRESS

Trace the pattern. Cut out the pieces, adding 6 mm ($^1/_4$ in) seam allowances to them all, except the three crazy patchwork bands and the two pocket pieces where a 1 cm ($^3/_8$ in) seam allowance is added. Add an additional 2 cm ($^3/_4$ in) down all the centre back edges for facings.

CRAZY PATCHWORK

Using the Narrow Strip method, crazy patch the three band pieces and the two pockets. We have not added any seam embroidery on the crazy pieces for this project, preferring the contrast between crazy patching and the calico dress. You could, of course, add as much, or as little, as you wish.

MAKING UP

STEP ONE

Cut two additional heart pockets from calico. With the right sides together, stitch a patchwork pocket to a calico pocket, leaving an opening where indicated. Trim the seams to 4 mm ($^3/_{16}$ in), clip the curves and turn the pockets right sides out. Press and set them aside.

STEP TWO

Note: No instructions are given for neatening seams. Oversewing, zigzagging or cutting with pinking shears are all acceptable. Neaten each seam with your preferred method.

Matching the numbered or lettered notches, join the dress, patchwork band and hem for the front and two back pieces.

STEP THREE

Pin the two heart pockets in place as indicated on the pattern. Stitch them in place, between the dots, with a row of feather stitch, using the rayon thread.

STEP FOUR

Stitch a line of gathering, as marked, along the top edge of the dress. Adjust it to fit and join it to the front and two back bodice pieces. Sew the backs to the front at the shoulders.

STEP FIVE

Sew a line of gathering at the top of the sleeve where indicated. Pull up the gathers and pin the sleeves into the sleeve openings. Adjust for a correct fit, then stitch the sleeves in place.

STEP SIX

With the right sides facing and matching the armhole seams and the edges of the band, stitch the dress together from the hem to the dot on the sleeve. Turn under 3 mm ($^3/_{16}$ in), then another 3 mm ($^3/_{16}$ in) of the remaining sleeve seam to form the placket. Baste the folds on the lower edges of the sleeves as indicated. With the right sides facing, pin one long side of the cuff to the lower edge of the sleeve. Stitch. Fold in the 6 mm ($^1/_4$ in) seam allowance on the remaining three sides of the cuff, then fold it over double. Stitch by hand as invisibly as possible.

STEP SEVEN

Turn under 6 mm (¹/₄ in) along the edge of the centre back. Turn a further 1 cm (³/₈ in) and press firmly. Stitch by hand as invisibly as possible.

STEP EIGHT

With the right sides facing, stitch two collar pieces together. Clip the curves, press, then turn the collar to the right side. Repeat for the other collar piece. With the right side of the dress and the underside of the collar facing, pin the collar pieces in place. Adjust, if necessary, then stitch. Apply bias binding to cover the seam allowances of collar and neck edge.

STEP NINE

Turn up 1 cm (³/₈ in) along the dress hem. Turn up the hem again, matching the folded edge with the stitching line where the band joins the dress. Stitch the hem invisibly in place.

STEP TEN

Lap the left side of the dress back over the right and attach four press studs evenly down the back. Stitch three buttons evenly down the centre front for decoration. Stitch a button on each cuff and work a button loop on the other side.

APRON

Note: This apron is not lined. If you wish to line it, follow the lining instruction for Teddy Bear's Vest on this page.

PREPARATION

See the pattern on the Pull Out Pattern Sheet.

Trace the pattern and transfer all the markings. Cut out the apron from the base cloth fabric allowing an extra 2.5 cm (1 in) all around. On the wrong side of the fabric, mark the stitching and cutting lines.

CRAZY PATCHWORK

STEP ONE

Using the Centre Patch method, crazy patch the apron. Machine a row of zigzag stitches along the cutting line, then trim any excess fabric. Hand-sew a row of basting on the stitching line.

STEP TWO

Add lace or braids to cover some of the seam lines. Cover all the remaining seam lines with your choice of embroidery stitches. Embellish these rows of stitches with beads or stitch combinations. Do not bead past the row of hand-basting.

STEP THREE

Add lace motifs, ribbon embroidery, beads and buttons to complete the decoration. Stitch your name and a message, if desired.

MAKING UP

STEP ONE

Turn under 6 mm (¹/₄ in) on one end of the bias binding. Starting mid-way down one of the back edges and with the right sides together, pin the bias binding to the apron, placing the seam fold exactly on top of the row of hand-basting. Using the zipper foot on the sewing machine, stitch the binding in place with the stitching line exactly on the fold line. Stitch slowly around the curves, clipping the binding, but not the fabric, for a smooth, rounded shape. Trim the seam allowance back to 6 mm (¹/₄ in), then slipstitch the other edge of binding to the row of stitches on the wrong side.

STEP TWO

Sew two press studs in place. On the front of the apron disguise the position of each press stud with a white button.

TEDDY BEAR'S VEST

PREPARATION

See the pattern on the Pull Out Pattern Sheet.

STEP ONE

Trace the pattern onto the white paper and transfer all the markings.

STEP TWO

Cut two vest fronts from the base cloth fabric allowing an extra 2.5 cm (1 in) all round. Make sure you cut a right and a left side. On the wrong side, mark the stitching and cutting lines. With the lining fabric folded right sides together, cut one front and two backs.

CRAZY PATCHWORK

STEP ONE

Using the Centre Patch method, crazy patch both the fronts, maintaining a balance of fabrics on each side. Machine a row of zigzag stitches along the cutting line and trim any excess fabric. Hand-sew a row of basting on the stitching line.

STEP TWO

Add lace or braids to cover some of the seam lines. Cover all the remaining seam lines with your choice of embroidery stitches. Embellish these rows of stitches with beads or stitch combinations. Do not bead past the row of hand-basting.

STEP THREE

Add lace motifs, ribbon embroidery, beads and buttons to complete the decoration. Stitch your name and a message, if desired.

MAKING UP

STEP ONE

Sew the darts on the back and the back linings. Press the back darts towards the centre back and the lining darts towards the armholes.

STEP TWO

Stitch the centre back seam on the back and on the lining. Clip the curves and press the seam open.

STEP THREE

Pin each vest front to each lining front, with the right sides together. Stitch around the armholes and from the neck edge down the fronts and across the bottom to the side seams. Clip the corners and curves, then press the seams open. Pull the vest through to the right side through the side seams.

STEP FOUR

Lay the vest back on the table with the right side up. Position the fronts on top with the right sides down, aligning the shoulder and side seams. Finally place the back lining on top, with the right side down, again aligning the shoulder and side seams. Take care that the points at the lower edge of the vest front do not poke through the seam line – pin them carefully out of the way, if necessary. Pin through all three pieces (four layers of fabric). Begin stitching 2 cm (^{3}/$_4$ in) past the centre back seam and sew along the remainder of one side of the lower back to the side seam, then up the side seam to the underarm. Sew the arm seam of the back (the front is already done) across the shoulder, back neck, other shoulder and down the other side, returning to a point 2 cm (^{3}/$_4$ in) from the centre back seam. You will have 4 cm (1^1/$_2$ in) of the lower back seam unsewn. Clip all the curves and remove any excess bulk from the shoulder seams. Press all the seams open, then pull the whole vest to the right side through the gap in the centre back seam. Press the vest and slipstitch the opening closed.

FRINGED COATHANGER

A variation on the padded coathanger, this fringed beauty would also make a lovely gift for a friend.

MATERIALS

White paper
Pencil
Adult-sized wooden coathanger
15 cm x 45 cm (6 in x 18 in) of fabric for the base cloth
15 cm x 45 cm (6 in x 18 in) of gold satin for the back
45 cm (18 in) of gold fringed braid
Total of 20 cm x 55 cm (8 in x 22 in) of scraps of six gold, mauve, and pale green fancy fabrics
20 cm (8 in) of wide cotton lace
20 cm (8 in) of narrow cotton lace or tatting
Stranded embroidery thread: Cream, Purple, Green, Gold
Ordinary sewing thread
Assorted beads and buttons
30 cm (12 in) of 7 mm ($5/16$ in) wide silk ribbon, Cream
10 cm (4 in) of 7 mm ($5/16$ in) wide silk ribbon, Mauve
Scraps of assorted other 3 mm ($3/16$ in) wide silk ribbons
15 cm (6 in) of tubular knitting ribbon or braid to cover the hook
30 cm (12 in) of flannelette, fleecy fabric or thin wadding
Crewel needle
Beading needle
Chenille needle
Craft glue

PREPARATION

See the pattern on the Pull Out Pattern Sheet.

Trace the pattern onto the white paper and transfer all the markings. Using the pattern, cut one coathanger from the base cloth fabric, allowing an extra 3 cm ($1\frac{1}{4}$ in) all round. On the wrong side, mark the stitching and cutting lines. Cut one coathanger from the gold satin and set it aside.

CRAZY PATCHWORK

STEP ONE

Using the Random Block or Narrow Strip method, crazy patch the coathanger front. Machine a row of zigzag stitching along the cutting line, then trim away any excess. Hand-sew a row of basting on the stitching line.

STEP TWO

Add lace or braids to cover some of the seam lines. Cover all the remaining seam lines with your choice of embroidery stitches. Embellish these rows of stitches with beads or stitch combinations. Do not bead past the row of hand-basting.

Silk roses and tea-dyed lace

MAKING UP

STEP ONE

Insert the hook into the wooden hanger. Cut the flannelette, fleecy fabric or wadding into strips about 5 cm (2 in) wide. Bind the wooden hanger tightly with these strips to pad it. Wind from the centre to one end, then back to the other end (past the hook), before returning to the hook. Secure the padding with a few stitches. This hanger is not heavily padded, but covering the wood makes the fabric sit better.

STEP TWO

Place the crazy patchwork front and satin back with the right sides together. Stitch from **X** to **X**, leaving an opening for the hook (as marked on the pattern). Reinforce the stitching on either side of the hook opening. Clip the seam and press it open. Turn the cover right side out.

STEP THREE

Remove the hook from the padded hanger and cover it with the tubular ribbon or braid. Place the padded hanger into the cover and reinsert the hook, securing the hook cover with a few tiny stitches.

STEP FOUR

Turn in the seam allowances on the lower edge and slipstitch them closed. Apply the fringed braid to the lower edge, stitching between the loops of the braid so that no stitches are visible. A dab of craft glue will stop the ends of the braid from fraying while you sew it on.

ACKNOWLEDGMENTS

It would not have been possible for us to write this book without the help and support of a number of people. We thank you all: Karen Fail and Judy Poulos from J.B. Fairfax for seeing the potential in our work; Andrew Payne, not only for his superb photography, but also for pointing us in the right direction!; Ainsley, Barbara, Bruno, Jean, Kristie, Lanika, Lauren, Robin, and Shannon, to whom many of the projects in this book now belong; Julie and Wanda for proofreading our instructions; and Audrey Clatworthy from The Sewing Basket for threads and encouragement.

A very special thanks to Tony and Bob, for their patience, encouragement and support.

Make this lovely blue teddy in the same way as the one on page 27